TASK FORCE MEMBERS

Task Force members are asked to join a consensus signifying that they endorse "the general policy thrust and judgments reached by the group, though not necessarily every finding and recommendation." They participate in the Task Force in their individual, not institutional, capacities.

Kevin M. Brown
Dell Technologies

Michèle A. Flournoy
WestExec Advisors

Susan M. Gordon
GordonVentures LLC

Harry Harris
U.S. Navy, Ret.

Paul Heer★
Chicago Council on Global Affairs

Charles Hooper
U.S. Army, Ret.

Ivan Kanapathy★
Edmund A. Walsh School of Foreign Service, Georgetown University

Patricia M. Kim★
The Brookings Institution

Margaret K. Lewis★
Seton Hall University School of Law

Chris Miller
The Fletcher School, Tufts University

Michael G. Mullen
U.S. Navy, Ret.

Meghan L. O'Sullivan
Harvard Kennedy School

Douglas H. Paal★
Carnegie Endowment for International Peace

Minxin Pei
Claremont McKenna College

Matt Pottinger★
Hoover Institution, Stanford University

Daniel R. Russel★
Asia Society

David Sacks
Council on Foreign Relations

W9-ATL-544

★The individual has endorsed the report and signed an additional or dissenting view.

Independent Task Force Report No. 81

U.S.-Taiwan Relations in a New Era

Responding to a More Assertive China

Susan M. Gordon and Michael G. Mullen, *Chairs*
David Sacks, *Project Director*

The Council on Foreign Relations (CFR) is an independent, nonpartisan membership organization, think tank, and publisher dedicated to being a resource for its members, government officials, business executives, journalists, educators and students, civic and religious leaders, and other interested citizens in order to help them better understand the world and the foreign policy choices facing the United States and other countries. Founded in 1921, CFR carries out its mission by maintaining a diverse membership, with special programs to promote interest and develop expertise in the next generation of foreign policy leaders; convening meetings at its headquarters in New York and in Washington, DC, and other cities where senior government officials, members of Congress, global leaders, and prominent thinkers come together with Council members to discuss and debate major international issues; supporting a Studies Program that fosters independent research, enabling CFR scholars to produce articles, reports, and books and hold roundtables that analyze foreign policy issues and make concrete policy recommendations; publishing *Foreign Affairs*, the preeminent journal on international affairs and U.S. foreign policy; sponsoring Independent Task Forces that produce reports with both findings and policy prescriptions on the most important foreign policy topics; and providing up-to-date information and analysis about world events and American foreign policy on its website, CFR.org.

The Council on Foreign Relations takes no institutional positions on policy issues and has no affiliation with the U.S. government. All views expressed in its publications and on its website are the sole responsibility of the author or authors.

The Council on Foreign Relations sponsors Independent Task Forces to assess issues of current and critical importance to U.S. foreign policy and provide policymakers with concrete judgments and recommendations. Diverse in backgrounds and perspectives, Task Force members aim to reach a meaningful consensus on policy through private deliberations. Once launched, Task Forces are independent of CFR and solely responsible for the content of their reports. Task Force members are asked to join a consensus signifying that they endorse "the general policy thrust and judgments reached by the group, though not necessarily every finding and recommendation." Each Task Force member also has the option of putting forward an additional or a dissenting view. Members' affiliations are listed for identification purposes only and do not imply institutional endorsement. Task Force observers participate in discussions, but are not asked to join the consensus.

For further information about CFR or this Task Force, please write to the Council on Foreign Relations, 58 East 68th Street, New York, NY 10065, or call the Communications office at 212.434.9888. Visit our website, CFR.org.

This report is printed on paper that is FSC® Chain-of-Custody Certified by a printer who is certified by BM TRADA North America Inc.

CONTENTS

FOREWORD

For decades, the United States, China, and Taiwan have successfully finessed the question of Taiwan's status. The three sides held differing views of Taiwan's relationship to China, but did not seek to resolve this question and did not challenge one another's bottom line. Through skillful diplomacy, the United States and China were able to set aside their fundamental disagreement over Taiwan and establish diplomatic ties, collaborate to counter the Soviet Union, and build mutually beneficial commercial relations. Paired with reassurances the United States provided to Taiwan, unique legal commitments under the Taiwan Relations Act, and a good measure of military deterrence, peace has held in the Taiwan Strait. This has allowed Taiwan to prosper, enabling a democratic transformation and a remarkable economic ascendance.

It is unclear, however, whether what has worked for five decades will work for another five years, much less another five decades. The biggest question revolves around China's ambitions and the aspirations of Chinese leader Xi Jinping. Xi has stated that the Taiwan issue cannot be passed on to future generations and has asserted that unification with Taiwan is the essence of China's national rejuvenation. Under Xi's leadership, Chinese foreign policy has become both more assertive and more prepared to accept risk, as evidenced by its militarization of the South China Sea, its economic coercion of countries, and its growing willingness to assert its territorial claims against its neighbors.

With respect to Taiwan, over the past decade China has dramatically increased military, economic, and diplomatic pressure, while also interfering in Taiwan's politics and conducting cyber and disinformation operations. This coercion is intended to wear down and demoralize the Taiwanese people, allowing China to achieve its political objectives without using force. At the same time, Xi is not taking any chances and has pushed through major military reforms that are intended to give him a viable military option for resolving the Taiwan question and, according to U.S. intelligence, has ordered the People's Liberation Army to be ready to invade the island by 2027. As China's economic growth slows and Xi looks to both maintain the Chinese Communist Party's hold on power and cement his personal legacy, he could see Taiwan as a tempting target.

China's pressure campaign against Taiwan and its crackdown on democracy in Hong Kong have led to growing disillusionment among the Taiwanese people. Public polling reveals that few Taiwanese want unification, while the share of those who identify as Chinese continues to decline. Prospects for peaceful unification are becoming increasingly remote, and if Xi decides that the status quo is unacceptable, he would likely have to use nonpeaceful means to achieve his objectives.

In the United States, a growing appreciation for Taiwan's strategic and economic importance and recognition of its democratic achievements have led to calls to upgrade U.S.-Taiwan relations. In recent years, the United States has dropped most restrictions on contact with Taiwan's officials, while security cooperation has increased and high-level visits have become more frequent. In joint statements with close allies, appeals to maintaining peace in the Taiwan Strait are now commonplace. While such steps arguably send an important signal to China regarding U.S. interests at stake, they also feed concern in Beijing that the trend lines are moving in an unfavorable direction, i.e., away from unification, and as a result increase China's sense of urgency.

The Task Force finds that the United States has vital strategic interests in the Taiwan Strait and outlines the stakes. If China were to annex Taiwan against the will of the Taiwanese people, it would undermine the most basic tenet of international order: that territory is not to be acquired through force. If China were to station its military on the island, it would gain power projection capabilities that would make it significantly more difficult for the United States to defend its allies. Should the United States fail to counter Chinese military aggression against Taiwan, its allies in the region would come to have grave doubts as to whether they could rely on the United States for their security and would then choose to either accommodate China or pursue strategic autonomy, which could include developing nuclear weapons. Given Taiwan's dominance in semiconductor production, a conflict in the Taiwan Strait would shave trillions of dollars off global economic output. Finally, if China were to take control of Taiwan, it would extinguish a liberal democracy.

This Task Force report deftly analyzes dynamics in Beijing, Taipei, and Washington and proposes policy options intended to reduce the chances of a calamitous conflict. Most fundamentally, it calls for maintaining the political status quo, which, while not ideal, remains the only option acceptable to all sides. It advocates for taking an array of steps to strengthen Taiwan as it faces a sophisticated effort to undermine its people's confidence. It warns that deterrence is at risk of failing and puts forward a host of recommendations to increase Taiwan's defensive capabilities and the ability of the United States, Japan, and others to come to Taiwan's defense. In so doing, what emerges is the notion that what has largely worked in aiding Ukraine against Russian aggression—namely, an indirect strategy of providing military and other support while sanctioning the aggressor—would not be sufficient here. The Task Force sensibly calls for avoiding symbolic gestures that do not strengthen Taiwan's security but make a conflict more likely. The report also urges the United States to do more to improve Americans' understanding of the stakes involved.

While the Task Force did not arrive at a unanimous view on the question of whether the United States should maintain strategic ambiguity or adopt strategic clarity and explicitly state that it would come to Taiwan's direct defense, it makes clear that the United States should do more to ensure that it has the ability to defend Taiwan in the face of a mounting threat. My own view is that strategic clarity is a necessary component of—and complement to—such steps and would bolster deterrence by erasing any doubts in the mind of Xi, as well as America's partners, that the United States would defend Taiwan.

This report treats one of the most complex, vexing issues in U.S. foreign policy with subtlety. Experts and nonexperts alike would benefit from reading this careful evaluation of one of the most consequential foreign policy questions facing the United States and how we arrived at this point. I thank the Task Force chairs, Mike Mullen and Sue Gordon, for their leadership and significant contributions to this project. My gratitude extends to all the Task Force members and observers for lending their knowledge and expertise, especially when their time is in such high demand. I also thank CFR's David Sacks, who directed the Task Force and authored this report, and Anya Schmemann, who guided the entire project as Task Force program director. They have all earned our gratitude for taking on this important subject.

Richard Haass
President
Council on Foreign Relations
June 2023

ACKNOWLEDGMENTS

This report is the result of the dedicated members and observers of the Independent Task Force on Taiwan, who devoted over six months to examining the profound changes underway in U.S.-Taiwan and cross-strait relations and to offering practical, realistic options for one of the world's most urgent foreign policy challenges. I am grateful for the time, attention, and expertise they provided.

I would especially like to thank our distinguished co-chairs, Admiral Michael G. Mullen and the Honorable Susan M. Gordon. Mike and Sue delivered steadfast leadership and expert guidance throughout the duration of the project. Their penetrating and challenging questions drove the report forward, while their insights strengthened every element. It was a privilege to work with them both.

Throughout this process, I was encouraged by the robust dialogue at our Task Force meetings and remain deeply grateful for the contributions of each Task Force member and observer. I would like to acknowledge Kevin Brown, Admiral Harry Harris, Paul Heer, Ivan Kanapathy, Chris Miller, Danny Russel, and Sheila Smith in particular for their detailed feedback on multiple drafts. I want to thank Ambassador Raymond Burghardt for training his keen eye on a draft of the report. I also thank Chris Miller and Matt Pottinger for delivering remarks at our Task Force meetings to frame our group discussions.

Thanks are due to several practitioners and experts outside the Task Force who generously lent their time and knowledge to our efforts, including Admiral John C. Aquilino, Richard C. Bush, Ely Ratner, and Laura Rosenberger. The report was also greatly informed by a research trip to Taiwan in early 2023, ably led by Sue Gordon and Harry Harris. I am grateful to the senior officials from Taiwan's National Security Council, Ministry of Foreign Affairs, Ministry of National Defense,

Ministry of Economic Affairs, and Ministry of Digital Affairs who met with our delegation and shared their unique perspectives on these evolving issues.

My special thanks go to the Taipei Economic and Cultural Office in New York, in particular Karen Chu, for helping to arrange our meetings, and to Taiwan's Ministry of Foreign Affairs for guiding us during our stay. I want to thank the American Institute in Taiwan for meeting with us and discussing the trajectory of U.S.-Taiwan relations. We also benefited from the opportunity to hear views from the Kuomintang's leadership. Although this report is the product of the Independent Task Force, and we sought the advice of many, I take responsibility for its ultimate content.

I also want to acknowledge the work of my colleagues at CFR, listed at the end of this report, who have made this report possible. The Product, Design, and Publications teams deserve credit for organizing and executing the production of this report. In particular, I thank Maria Teresa Alzuru, Michael Bricknell, and Will Merrow for their hard work on the data visualizations that help the report come to life. I am thankful for the diligent research of David Brostoff, Addis Goldman, Seaton Huang, and Claire Tiunn (Chang). Chelie Setzer and Connor Sutherland of the Independent Task Force Program were instrumental in the smooth operation of every aspect of this process; in particular, I want to single out the detailed edits they offered to multiple drafts. I would like to thank Anya Schmemann, managing director of the Independent Task Force Program, who guided this project from start to finish and provided valuable input on both the content and form of the report.

Last but certainly not least, I thank CFR President Richard Haass for giving me the opportunity to direct this important and timely project and supporting the endeavor along the way.

David Sacks
Project Director

INDEPENDENT
TASK FORCE REPORT

EXECUTIVE SUMMARY

A conflict between the United States and the People's Republic of China (PRC, or China) over Taiwan is becoming increasingly imaginable, a result of China's growing military capabilities and assertiveness, the emergence and coalescence of a separate Taiwanese identity, and evolving U.S. calculations about its interests at stake in the Taiwan Strait. If deterrence fails and a war erupts, the result would be calamitous for Taiwan, China, the United States, and the world, resulting in thousands of casualties on all sides and a profound global economic depression.

The United States has critical strategic interests in the Taiwan Strait. If China were to successfully annex Taiwan against the will of the Taiwanese people, doing so on the heels of Russia's invasion of Ukraine, it would severely undermine international order by again demonstrating that countries can use coercion or force to unilaterally redraw borders. If China were to station its military on the island, the United States would find it far more difficult to project power, defend its treaty allies, and operate in international waters in the Western Pacific. U.S. influence would wane because its allies would question U.S. commitment to their defense and either accommodate China or pursue strategic autonomy. A war in the Taiwan Strait would also halt the production and shipment of the majority of the world's semiconductors, paralyzing global supply chains and ushering in a severe economic crisis. Finally, if China were to take control of Taiwan, it would spell the end of a liberal democracy and have chilling effects on democracies around the world. The Task Force thus finds that it is vital for the United States to deter China from using force or coercion to achieve unification with Taiwan.

The Task Force assesses that although China is developing the military capabilities it would need to annex Taiwan and is determined to subjugate the island, it has not yet decided to pursue a nonpeaceful res-olution and deterrence remains possible. Although war is not inevita-ble, unless the United States moves with urgency to bolster deterrence and shape Chinese leader Xi Jinping's decision-making calculus to raise the costs of aggressive action against Taiwan, the odds of a conflict will increase.

Reinforcing deterrence without provoking the conflict that it seeks to avoid is no small task. Indeed, some argue that, given the risk, the United States should lessen its support for Taiwan. Such a course, how-ever, fails to adequately reckon with what the world would look like the day after a successful Chinese assault: markedly less safe, less free, and less prosperous. Beyond deterring Chinese aggression, the United States also has an interest in enhancing its unofficial relationship with a top-ten trading partner, a fellow democracy, and a like-minded force on global issues.

The Task Force finds that the political framework established more than four decades ago, whereby Taiwan, China, and the United States all embrace different conceptions of Taiwan's relationship to China but do not explicitly challenge one another's position, is becoming more and more brittle. This reality, paired with Xi's unease with the status quo and his determination to make progress toward unification, increases the risk of a conflict. In particular, the Task Force finds that

- the prevailing political framework has allowed for peace and stability in the Taiwan Strait while enabling rapid economic growth in both Taiwan and China;

- the status quo is under increasing strain as China, Taiwan, and the United States reevaluate whether the long-standing political formula-tion continues to serve their respective interests;

- the likelihood of resolving cross-strait differences peacefully is steadily decreasing;

- as the prospect of achieving peaceful unification grows more remote, China will increasingly employ coercive tools against Taiwan; and

- the chance of a conflict will rise as Xi Jinping approaches the end of his tenure and the basis of his legitimacy shifts from delivering economic growth to satisfying Chinese nationalism.

The Task Force analyzed how Taiwan's role as the primary producer of the world's semiconductors, including nearly all of the most advanced chips, would affect deterrence and China's calculus. The Task Force concludes that although China's reliance on chips manufactured in Taiwan would raise the costs of a conflict, it does not act as a "silicon shield" that can protect Taiwan from an attack. The greater danger is that China will be able to leverage economic interdependence to deter countries from coming to Taiwan's direct or indirect defense. The Task Force finds that

- Taiwan's critical role in global supply chains—above all, semiconductor production—acts as a brake to hostilities but does not diminish China's desire to gain control over Taiwan;

- in addition to the devastation for the people of Taiwan, a conflict would also trigger a global economic depression and open-ended era of hostility between the world's two leading powers;

- Taiwan's dependence on trade with China provides Beijing with leverage over Taipei that could reduce the latter's options during a crisis;

- U.S. and allied reliance on semiconductors produced in Taiwan raises the stakes for the United States and the West in a conflict; and

- U.S. and allied economic interdependence with China would complicate efforts to resist Chinese aggression against Taiwan and impose costs on Beijing.

The Task Force asserts that the United States has not only legal but also vital strategic reasons for maintaining the capacity to come to Taiwan's direct defense. At the same time, however, China's rapid military modernization, Taiwan's underinvestment in its military, and U.S. military gaps mean that the United States cannot assume that it would be able to decisively intervene on Taiwan's behalf. The Task Force finds that

- deterrence is steadily eroding in the Taiwan Strait and is at risk of failing, increasing the likelihood of Chinese aggression;

- China does not yet have the ability to invade and seize Taiwan in the face of U.S. intervention, but, barring a significant transformation of Taiwan's military and sustained focus from the U.S. Department of Defense (DOD), it will likely gain the capability to do so by the end of the decade;

- despite some progress, Taiwan is still not doing enough to address critical shortfalls in its defense and civil resilience;

- the United States has major military gaps that it is addressing but that would nonetheless make coming to Taiwan's defense difficult and costly; and

- support from allies and partners will be imperative for a U.S. defense of Taiwan, but the level of assistance the United States can expect is largely unknown.

The Task Force recommends that U.S. diplomacy focus on preserving the political foundation that has worked for decades but has become increasingly challenged by all sides. U.S. diplomacy should aim to deter Chinese aggression, signal to China and Taiwan that it opposes unilateral changes to the status quo, and ensure that any future arrangement between China and Taiwan be arrived at peacefully and with the assent of the Taiwanese people. In support of these objectives, the United States should

- maintain its One China policy, recognizing the PRC as the sole legal government of China and eschewing formal diplomatic relations with Taiwan while fulfilling its unique legal commitments to the island, and emphasize that such a policy is predicated on China pursuing a peaceful resolution of cross-strait issues;

- avoid symbolic political and diplomatic gestures that provoke a Chinese response but do not meaningfully improve Taiwan's defensive capabilities, resilience, or economic competitiveness;

- explain to the American people why Taiwan matters and why they should care about its fate;

- create additional international and multilateral forums that allow Taiwan to have its voice heard and contribute to resolving global issues, in a way that does not suggest Taiwanese independence; and

- promote people-to-people ties between the United States and Taiwan.

The United States should assist Taiwan in reducing its economic dependence on the PRC and bolstering its integration into the global economy, which would improve Taiwan's ability to withstand China's economic coercion. In addition, given its heavy reliance on Taiwan for semiconductor manufacturing, the United States needs to ensure that Taiwan remains a trusted economic and trading partner. In particular, the Task Force recommends that the United States

- negotiate a bilateral trade agreement with Taiwan;

- diversify supply chains in critical sectors to reduce the risk from potential Chinese economic retaliation;

- build resiliency in global semiconductor manufacturing;

- raise awareness of the economic consequences of a Chinese blockade or attack on Taiwan with allies and partners and coordinate with them to prepare sanctions on China; and

- work with Taiwan to reduce the PRC's economic leverage and respond to its economic coercion.

The Task Force maintains that deterring Chinese aggression against Taiwan should be the United States' top priority in the Indo-Pacific. As a core objective, the United States should ensure that every time Chinese leaders look across the Taiwan Strait, they conclude that a blockade or invasion would fail and that pursuing such a course would make it impossible for them to accomplish China's modernization objectives. Achieving this goal will be difficult but doable with the correct mix of policies. To accomplish it, the Task Force recommends that the United States

- prioritize Taiwan contingencies as the DOD pacing scenario and ensure DOD spending supports capabilities and initiatives critical to success, securing the United States' ability to effectively come to Taiwan's defense;

- fundamentally shift U.S.-Taiwan security relations to build Taiwan's self-defense capabilities;

- seek greater clarity from allies on the assistance they would provide during Taiwan contingencies and work to improve their capabilities and define their roles and responsibilities;

- place the U.S. defense industrial base on a wartime footing now to ensure that the U.S. military has the capabilities it needs to deter Chinese aggression and prioritize arms deliveries to Taiwan; and

- conduct a joint study with Taiwan of its war reserve munitions, ability to produce weapons during wartime, and stockpile of essential goods.

U.S. policy toward Taiwan needs to evolve to contend with a more capable, assertive, and risk-acceptant China that is increasingly dissatisfied with the status quo. Making long overdue adjustments will be difficult, but a failure to adapt is far more dangerous. The future of the world's most economically critical region could very well hinge on whether the United States succeeds in deterring China and maintaining peace in the Taiwan Strait.

INTRODUCTION

For more than six decades, a tenuous peace has prevailed in the Taiwan Strait, enabling Taiwan's democratic transformation and economic ascendance, and allowing the United States to build productive commercial relations with the PRC and a close partnership with Taiwan. It is no longer clear, however, that what has worked will continue to do so. China has grown stronger and more assertive throughout the region, indeed the world, while the Taiwanese people have consolidated a separate identity and are yearning for international recognition and participation. In the United States, there are growing calls to either recognize Taiwan as a sovereign, independent country or otherwise safeguard its current de facto independent status.[1]

As relations between the United States and the PRC deteriorate and enter a new, more perilous era, Taiwan stands as the issue most likely to bring the two nuclear-armed powers and the world's two largest economies to a direct military confrontation. If such a conflict were to erupt, the United States and China would likely be involved in a war marked by the most intense fighting since World War II, with thousands of casualties on both sides and almost incalculable global economic consequences.[2] Given the emotional weight that China attaches to Taiwan, Taiwan's role in modern Chinese nationalism, and the Chinese Communist Party (CCP) definition of Taiwan as a core interest, once a war starts, it would be difficult to terminate or deescalate. The stakes are enormous, and no one would win.

Russia's invasion of Ukraine serves as a reminder that war is not a relic of the past but is instead a tool that countries continue to employ to satisfy their territorial ambitions. It also demonstrates that authoritarian leaders with few internal political constraints can and will bear substantial economic, societal, and reputational costs to pursue their legacies and accomplish geopolitical objectives. The post–Cold War era has drawn to a close, replaced by an era of great power competition and potentially great power conflict, with Taiwan being the most probable flashpoint.

A conflict over Taiwan has thus far been avoided, but deterrence has dangerously eroded; under Xi Jinping's leadership, China is aggressively and consistently moving the status quo in its favor and increasing pressure on Taiwan. The Task Force thus believes that although a military confrontation in the Taiwan Strait is by no means inevitable, the United States and China are drifting toward a war over Taiwan. To avoid such an outcome, the United States must restore balance to a situation that has been allowed to tilt far too much in China's favor.

Reinforcing deterrence without escalating an already tense situation will be difficult. Given this risk, some analysts argue for reduced U.S. support for Taiwan and acquiescence to China's wishes. Abandoning a long-time partner and vibrant democracy of twenty-three million people located at a critical position in the world's most economically important region, however, would be an act of strategic malpractice and moral bankruptcy. The Task Force finds that a failure to deter China from seeking to forcefully annex Taiwan would damage an array of important, even vital, U.S. interests:

- **Global order:** In the wake of Russia's invasion of Ukraine, if China were to absorb Taiwan against the will of the Taiwanese people, it would be yet another demonstration that countries can unilaterally redraw borders, further undermining the most basic tenet of international rules and norms. Such an occurrence would likely embolden other countries with revanchist aims and reinforce Russia's position.

- **Security:** If the PRC were to gain control of Taiwan and station its military on the island, it would be able to project power far beyond the first island chain, which stretches from Japan through Taiwan and down to the Philippines. With the first island chain broken, the United States would effectively lose the ability to operate freely in international waters in the Western Pacific and would find it significantly more difficult to defend its Indo-Pacific allies.

- **Alliances:** Should the United States fail to counter Chinese military aggression against Taiwan, its allies in the region would come to have grave doubts as to whether they could rely on the United States for their security, especially extended deterrence. They would then have to choose to either accommodate China or pursue strategic autonomy—potentially to include developing nuclear weapons—either of which would result in diminished U.S. influence.

- **Economic stability and prosperity:** A conflict in the Taiwan Strait, regardless of whether the United States chose to intervene on Taiwan's behalf, would trigger an immediate and prolonged worldwide economic depression and shave trillions of dollars off economic output. Given Taiwan's dominant position in the global semiconductor industry, most companies would struggle to make much of anything that contains technology, which would profoundly disrupt people's lives throughout the world.

- **Democracy:** If the PRC were to take control of Taiwan, whether by force or coercion, it would extinguish a liberal democracy, with chilling effects on societies around the world.

The Task Force concludes that it is vital for the United States to deter China from using force or coercion to achieve unification with Taiwan, to fulfill its legal commitments to Taiwan under the Taiwan Relations Act (TRA), and to support a close democratic partner that is under immense threat.

History of U.S. Policy

The island of Taiwan has a complex history marked by the interplay between Indigenous groups and multiple colonial powers, from the Dutch to the Japanese, as well as a fluid and now fraught relationship with China (see figure 1). On the periphery of China's dynastic rule, Taiwan was only settled by China toward the end of its imperial history. Significant numbers of Chinese settlers first arrived in the sixteenth century, and the island was annexed in 1684.

The Qing dynasty exercised loose control over Taiwan until 1895, when it was forced to cede the island to Japan following its defeat in the Sino-Japanese War. This loss laid bare the Qing dynasty's failure to modernize and sparked a series of popular uprisings that overthrew imperial rule and led to the founding of the Republic of China (ROC) in 1912. Sun Yat-sen, the founder of the ROC, led the Nationalists, or Kuomintang (KMT), which became the country's ruling party. Following Sun's death in 1925, Chiang Kai-shek took the mantle of leadership but struggled to build a modern Chinese state in the following decades, which offered Mao Zedong and his Communist followers an opportunity to exploit growing disaffection and build a base of support.

Following Japan's attack on Pearl Harbor in 1941, the United States formed an alliance with the ROC, with Chiang committing substantial military forces to fighting the Japanese a move that enabled the United States to turn its attention first to the European theater. As Chiang's ally, President Franklin D. Roosevelt endorsed his stance that Taiwan, which had at this point been ruled by Japan for close to fifty years, should be returned to China following the war, a position that was formalized in the Cairo Declaration of 1943.[3] President Harry S. Truman took this same stance in the Potsdam Declaration of 1945.[4] After Japan's surrender, the KMT began to administer the island.

Figure 1

Taiwan and the Surrounding Region

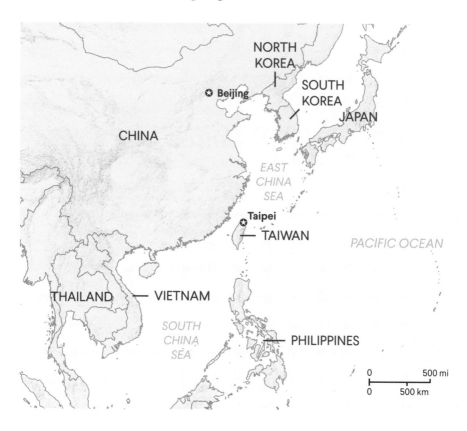

As another consequence of its alignment with Chiang, the United States became enmeshed in the Chinese Civil War, which pitted Chiang's KMT against Mao's Communists and broke into the open following World War II.[5] The United States at one point sought to mediate an end to the political struggle, with Truman dispatching General George Marshall on an unsuccessful mission to China to negotiate a peace between the two sides.[6] In Taiwan, disaffection with KMT rule grew, culminating in a large-scale uprising on February 28, 1947. The government responded by killing thousands of civilians in what become known as the February 28 massacre, or simply 228.

The United States eventually became disillusioned with Chiang as profound disagreements arose over his military strategy and approach to dealing with the Communist insurgency. The Truman administration concluded that no level of support short of a direct military intervention on Chiang's side could prevent a Communist takeover and decided to cut its losses. Chiang and his followers fled to Taiwan, where they hoped to regroup and retake the mainland (see figure 2).

Chiang's decision to relocate his government to Taiwan imbued the island with symbolic significance for Mao and the newly established PRC. Indeed, the CCP views Taiwan's continued separation as a reminder that its civil war remains unfinished and as an injustice that it continues to bear because it was weak in the face of foreign aggression. For Beijing, the Taiwan issue is a question of sovereignty, "the core of the core interests of China" that is not subject to negotiation.[7] The PRC, through its One China principle, argues that "there is only one China in the world, Taiwan is a part of China, and the government of the PRC is the sole legal government representing the whole of China."[8] CCP propaganda asserts that Taiwan is a lost piece of territory that must be returned to China in order for the latter to be restored to its former glory. Taiwan continues to occupy a unique place in the minds of PRC citizens and leaders, remaining deeply entwined with Chinese nationalism and national identity. Given the stakes that the CCP has associated with this issue, any Chinese leader would conclude that "losing" Taiwan through a unilateral declaration of independence under the name "Taiwan" would be politically unacceptable and potentially even fatal.

The United States resigned itself to Mao's forces absorbing Taiwan at some point, with Truman signaling in January 1950 that the United States would not intervene to prevent such an outcome.[9] North Korea's invasion of South Korea just months later in June 1950, however, fundamentally changed the U.S. calculus—and ultimately the course of Taiwan's history. In the wake of a Communist invasion of South Korea backed by Mao and Soviet leader Joseph Stalin, Truman declared that "the occupation of Formosa [a historical name for the island] by Communist forces would be a direct threat to the security of the Pacific area and to United States forces performing their lawful and necessary functions in that area."[10] Pursuant to this determination, he ordered the Seventh Fleet into the Taiwan Strait to prevent both Mao and Chiang from using the war as an opportunity to mount another attack. Reflecting on the pivotal role that these events played, U.S. National Security Advisor Henry Kissinger later remarked to PRC Premier Zhou Enlai, "There's no question that if the Korean War hadn't occurred...Taiwan would probably be today a part of the PRC."[11]

Just days after the Korean War erupted, on June 27, 1950, the Truman administration also shifted the official U.S. position on Taiwan's status, declaring, "The determination of the future status of Formosa must await the restoration of security in the Pacific, a peace settlement with Japan, or consideration by the United Nations."[12] The United States emphasized that Taiwan's legal status had not yet been determined (a position the United States continues to hold). This stance was embodied in the 1951 Treaty of San Francisco, in which Japan renounced its claim to Taiwan, but the inheritor of this claim was left ambiguous. As the Cold War solidified, Chiang came to be seen as a bulwark against Communism, with the United States stationing forces in Taiwan and providing the island with substantial economic aid. In 1954, following the PRC's shelling of Taiwan's offshore islands, the Dwight D. Eisenhower administration signed a mutual defense treaty with the ROC.

Although Chiang was perceived as an important partner in fighting Communism, he was in no way a democrat. Instead, he imposed martial law, arguing that the move was necessary given the ongoing fight against the Communists. The KMT government jailed and executed political dissidents during a decades-long period that became known as the White Terror. Native Taiwanese had almost no say in their governance because Chiang claimed to represent all of China, of which Taiwan was just a small part, and he used this justification to limit their political power. Though many Americans were uncomfortable with Chiang's repressive governance, Washington continued to support him as a partner in the Cold War. Later, the United States would play an important role in pressing Chiang's government to loosen its control over the population and adopt political reforms.

The formal alliance between the United States and the ROC began to fray as it became harder to maintain the fictions that Chiang represented all of China or that Mao's Communist regime would collapse. The decisive factor in the next major evolution of U.S.-Taiwan and cross-strait relations, however, was the growing convergence between Washington and Beijing on the need to counter the Soviet Union. As the Sino-Soviet split burst into the open, President Richard M. Nixon saw an opportunity to pursue a rapprochement with the PRC based on their shared enmity toward the Soviet Union.

The United States viewed Taiwan as one of many issues to discuss with the PRC during the normalization process, but it was by far the most important to the PRC. The PRC made clear that it was prepared to abandon normalization and forgo any strategic cooperation with the United States unless it broke diplomatic ties with Taiwan. The United

States sought a formula that would enable it to maintain some form of official relationship with Taiwan, such as a liaison office or consulate in Taipei, as well as a commitment from the PRC to resolve cross-strait issues peacefully, but the PRC flatly rejected such a proposal. Instead, it insisted that the United States withdraw its recognition of the ROC, terminate its mutual defense treaty, and remove all U.S. military personnel from the island, arguing that it was up to the Chinese how to resolve this "internal affair."[13]

The United States viewed Taiwan as one of many issues to discuss with the PRC during the normalization process, but it was by far the most important to the PRC.

Although they were unable to settle these fundamental differences, in 1972 the United States and China negotiated what became known as the Shanghai Communiqué, in which the two sides finessed their positions in a way that both could accept. In this communiqué, the United States "acknowledges that all Chinese on either side of the Taiwan Strait maintain there is but one China and that Taiwan is a part of China. The United States Government does not challenge that position. It reaffirms its interest in a peaceful settlement of the Taiwan question by the Chinese themselves."

The wording of each clause is significant and deserves further scrutiny. The United States took note of—or "acknowledged"—the Chinese position that Taiwan was a part of China without agreeing with or endorsing it. The communiqué noted that "all Chinese on either side of the Taiwan Strait" held this position, gesturing to the fact that Chiang and Mao both took this view that Taiwan was a part of China. Importantly, however, there is no mention of Taiwanese views on this question, as their voices were excluded during this period of authoritarian rule. The United States also agreed not to challenge the Chinese position on Taiwan, in essence forgoing a policy of "One China, One Taiwan" or "Two Chinas." Finally, by reaffirming its interest in a peaceful resolution of cross-strait differences by the two sides, the United States signaled its expectation that force would not be used and that it had no desire to mediate this dispute.

Following years of stalled negotiations, on December 15, 1978, the Jimmy Carter administration issued a communiqué announcing the establishment of diplomatic relations between the United States and PRC, which went into effect on January 1, 1979 (see figure 2).[14] The United States severed diplomatic ties with the ROC and recognized "the Government of the People's Republic of China as the sole legal Government of China." Washington again acknowledged—but did not recognize—Beijing's position that there is one China and that Taiwan is part of China. The United States also terminated its mutual defense treaty with Taiwan and committed to removing its military forces from the island. At the same time, however, the United States did not agree to stop selling defensive arms to Taiwan, nor did it renounce the right to come to Taiwan's defense.

The U.S. Congress, in part due to its resentment at being left out of the normalization process and the Carter administration's decision to abrogate a treaty without going through legislative channels, took the lead in crafting what the United States' unofficial relationship with Taiwan would look like. It dramatically altered the legislation that the Carter administration envisioned into something approaching a security guarantee. The Taiwan Relations Act, signed into law in 1979, established a nonprofit corporation, the American Institute in Taiwan (AIT), to oversee cultural, commercial, and other unofficial relations with the people of Taiwan.[15] In addition, the TRA asserts that it is U.S. policy to

- declare that peace and stability in the area are in the political, security, and economic interests of the United States, and are matters of international concern;

- make clear that the United States' decision to establish diplomatic relations with the PRC rests upon the expectation that the future of Taiwan will be determined by peaceful means;

- consider any effort to determine the future of Taiwan by other than peaceful means, including by boycotts or embargoes, a threat to the peace and security of the Western Pacific area and of grave concern to the United States;

- provide Taiwan with arms of a defensive character; and

- maintain the capacity of the United States to resist any resort to force or other forms of coercion that would jeopardize the security, or the social or economic system, of the people on Taiwan.

During negotiations with the PRC, Washington was unable to secure a pledge from Beijing that it would not use force against Taiwan. In the absence of that, the TRA makes an explicit linkage between the decision to establish diplomatic ties with the PRC and its handling of cross-strait issues. Although the TRA does not commit the United States to come to Taiwan's defense, it obligates the United States to maintain the capacity to do so. It also asserts a U.S. interest in peace and stability in the Taiwan Strait and notes that a use of force, boycott, or embargo against Taiwan would be "of grave concern to the United States," leaving the door open for U.S. intervention.

One major sticking point during negotiations over normalization was whether the United States would continue to sell arms to Taiwan. Although Beijing moved forward with normalization despite its objections to U.S. arms sales, it continued to seek a resolution on this matter. Thus the Ronald Reagan administration negotiated a communiqué with China in 1982 to address this issue. In this communiqué, the United States stated that it "does not seek to carry out a long-term policy of arms sales to Taiwan, that its arms sales to Taiwan will not exceed, either in qualitative or in quantitative terms, the level of those supplied in recent years since the establishment of diplomatic relations between the United States and China, and that it intends gradually to reduce its sale of arms to Taiwan, leading, over a period of time, to a final resolution." In addition, the United States stated explicitly for the first time that it "has no intention of...pursuing a policy of 'two Chinas' or 'one China, one Taiwan.'" [16]

President Reagan outlined his understanding of the communiqué in an internal memorandum, noting that "the U.S. willingness to reduce its arms sales to Taiwan is conditioned absolutely upon the continued commitment of China to the peaceful solution of the Taiwan-PRC differences. It should be clearly understood that the linkage between these two matters is a permanent imperative of U.S. foreign policy. In addition, it is essential that the quality and quantity of the arms provided Taiwan be conditioned entirely on the threat posed by the PRC. Both in quantitative and qualitative terms, Taiwan's defense capability relative to that of the PRC will be maintained."

Thus the cross-strait military balance would inform U.S. arms sales decisions; if China built up its forces targeting Taiwan, U.S. arms sales to Taiwan would not decline. Reagan also penned a private letter to Deng Xiaoping, then China's paramount leader, reiterating that "the United States has an abiding interest in the peaceful resolution of the Taiwan question." [17] The assertion of an "abiding interest" in the

Taiwan Strait signaled again to China that the United States reserved the right to intervene on Taiwan's behalf if the PRC used force. Importantly, however, Reagan's memorandum and letter represent unilateral interpretations that were never negotiated with or accepted by the PRC.

Attempting to allay concerns in Taipei, the Reagan administration in August 1982 privately conveyed to Taiwan assurances of what the United States had *not* agreed to in its negotiations with China, which became known as the Six Assurances.[18] In particular, the United States

- had not agreed to set a date for ending arms sales to Taiwan;

- had not agreed to consult with the PRC on arms sales to Taiwan;

- will not play any mediation role between Taipei and Beijing;

- had not agreed to revise the Taiwan Relations Act;

- had not agreed to take any position regarding sovereignty over Taiwan; and

- will not pressure Taiwan to negotiate with the PRC.

For nearly four decades, the Six Assurances and Reagan's internal memorandum remained classified, assuming an almost mythical quality. Debates raged about the tenses used in each assurance. Now that they have been declassified, what is clear is that most of the assurances spoke about what the United States *had not* agreed to when it negotiated the third communiqué with China, rather than what it *would not* agree to. [19] The third and sixth assurances, however, make unequivocal statements about enduring U.S. policy, noting that Washington would not pressure Taipei to enter into negotiations with Beijing or mediate this dispute.

Taken together, the three U.S.-China joint communiqués, the TRA, and the Six Assurances are referred to in shorthand as the One China policy.[20] Under its One China policy, the United States

- recognizes the PRC as the sole legal government of China and does not maintain formal diplomatic relations with Taiwan;

- acknowledges (but does not accept or endorse) the PRC claim that there is one China, of which Taiwan is a part, while simultaneously pledging not to challenge China's view or enact policies that are inconsistent with a one China framework (i.e., support for "two Chinas" or "one China, one Taiwan");

- does not take a position regarding sovereignty over Taiwan and views its status as undetermined;

- does not take a position on what any resolution of cross-strait differences should look like, instead prioritizing process, in particular that any outcome needs to be arrived at peacefully;

- asserts an interest in peace and stability in the Taiwan Strait, leaving open the possibility of intervening militarily on Taiwan's behalf;

- commits to providing Taiwan with weapons that enable it to maintain a sufficient self-defense capability; and

- makes a linkage between its One China policy and diplomatic ties with the PRC and Beijing's continued nonuse of force against Taiwan.[21]

Two additional, important elements have been added to the U.S. One China policy over time. First, in a nod to Taiwan's democratization, President Bill Clinton asserted that cross-strait issues "must be resolved peacefully and with the assent of the people of Taiwan."[22] This formulation makes clear that the United States would not support a settlement that is imposed on the Taiwanese. Clinton also became the first president to explicitly state that the United States does not support Taiwan's independence, while also adding that the United States does not believe that Taiwan should be a member in any international organization in which statehood is a requirement.[23] This statement was intended to signal to Taiwan that it did not have a blank check and that U.S. support would be conditional on Taiwan not provoking the PRC.

Although Washington's One China policy provides a broad framework for defining and conducting U.S.-Taiwan relations, it leaves room for policymakers to use their discretion to determine which actions are consistent with this policy. For instance, following the Taiwan Policy Review in 1994, AIT personnel began attending meetings in Taiwan's government buildings, and cabinet-level U.S. officials could travel to Taiwan on a case-by-case basis. The United States also chose to take a more active role in supporting Taiwan's participation in international organizations (although it would not support Taiwan's full membership

Figure 2

Major Events in Cross-Strait and Modern U.S.-Taiwan Relations

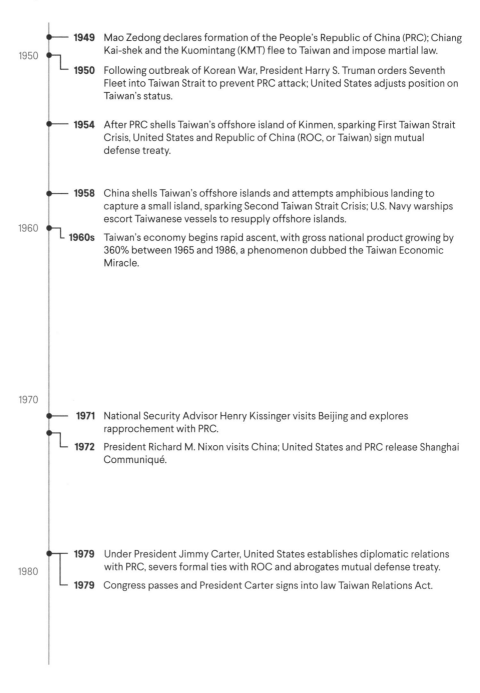

1950

1949 Mao Zedong declares formation of the People's Republic of China (PRC); Chiang Kai-shek and the Kuomintang (KMT) flee to Taiwan and impose martial law.

1950 Following outbreak of Korean War, President Harry S. Truman orders Seventh Fleet into Taiwan Strait to prevent PRC attack; United States adjusts position on Taiwan's status.

1954 After PRC shells Taiwan's offshore island of Kinmen, sparking First Taiwan Strait Crisis, United States and Republic of China (ROC, or Taiwan) sign mutual defense treaty.

1958 China shells Taiwan's offshore islands and attempts amphibious landing to capture a small island, sparking Second Taiwan Strait Crisis; U.S. Navy warships escort Taiwanese vessels to resupply offshore islands.

1960

1960s Taiwan's economy begins rapid ascent, with gross national product growing by 360% between 1965 and 1986, a phenomenon dubbed the Taiwan Economic Miracle.

1970

1971 National Security Advisor Henry Kissinger visits Beijing and explores rapprochement with PRC.

1972 President Richard M. Nixon visits China; United States and PRC release Shanghai Communiqué.

1979 Under President Jimmy Carter, United States establishes diplomatic relations with PRC, severs formal ties with ROC and abrogates mutual defense treaty.

1980

1979 Congress passes and President Carter signs into law Taiwan Relations Act.

1987 Taiwan President Chiang Ching-kuo lifts martial law and begins democratization process in Taiwan.

1990

1995 Taiwan President Lee Teng-hui gives speech at Cornell University, sparking Third Taiwan Strait Crisis.

1996 Taiwan holds first direct presidential election.

2000

2000 Taiwan's main opposition party, the Democratic Progressive Party (DPP), assumes power for first time.

2008 Taiwan President Chen Shui-bian of the DPP pursues referendum seeking UN membership, despite protests from the United States and China.

2010

2008 The KMT's Ma Ying-jeou assumes presidency, seeks rapprochement with PRC on basis of 1992 Consensus.

2014 Sunflower Movement, protesting closer ties with the PRC, erupts in Taiwan.

2014 Chinese leader Xi Jinping links unification with Taiwan to "rejuvenation" of the Chinese nation, which must be achieved by 2049.

2016 The DPP's Tsai Ing-wen assumes presidency and does not endorse 1992 Consensus; PRC breaks off communications.

2020

2022 House Speaker Nancy Pelosi visits Taiwan; China responds with major military exercises.

2023 United States assesses that Xi has ordered the People's Liberation Army to be ready for an invasion of Taiwan by 2027.

Source: CFR research.

if the organization required statehood to join). Beginning in 2003, U.S. Foreign Service officers no longer had to resign from the State Department before joining AIT, and a few years later, active-duty military officers began serving at AIT (rather than just retired military personnel).[24] In 2020–21, the Donald Trump and Joe Biden administrations revised the guidelines that regulated executive branch contact with Taiwan's representatives in Washington to make them the least restrictive they had been in practice since 1979. These moves reflect a bipartisan consensus that Taiwan should be viewed as an important partner in its own right, rather than as a troublesome aspect of U.S.-China relations.

The U.S. One China policy has evolved over time and can be expected to continue to do so as dynamics in the Taiwan Strait change. One constant throughout this history, however, has been the U.S. desire to moderate or balance the most extreme impulses of both sides. This conviction has meant signaling to Beijing that it would pay an enormous price if it attempted to resolve cross-strait differences coercively—potentially to include direct U.S. military intervention—while also stressing to Taiwan that it cannot act with impunity. The question going forward is what approach is most likely to ensure cross-strait stability in the context of a more powerful and assertive China.

FINDINGS
Politics and Diplomacy

The prevailing political framework established over four decades ago has allowed for peace and stability in the Taiwan Strait while enabling rapid economic growth in both Taiwan and China.

Driven by the strategic imperative of working with Beijing to contain Moscow, the United States sought a rapprochement with China in the early 1970s. The thorniest issue between the two sides was Taiwan, which they never resolved but successfully finessed in the Shanghai Communiqué (1972) and the Normalization Communiqué (1979). Although President Nixon and his national security advisor, Henry Kissinger, privately came closer to Beijing's position on Taiwan, in these documents the United States acknowledged but did not recognize or endorse the PRC's view that Taiwan is a part of China.[25]

Even though the PRC did not achieve its objective of having the United States adopt its position on Taiwan, its leaders displayed pragmatism and patience.[26] China's willingness to accept fundamental differences over Taiwan's status as long as the United States did not explicitly challenge China's position and Taiwan did not pursue independence reflected the reality that, even if it wanted to use force, it did not have the requisite military capabilities. In addition, at the time of normalization, China's priority was modernizing its economy and it desperately needed U.S. investment to do so.

Equally important was the fact that Taiwan's leadership agreed with the PRC that Taiwan was a part of China, only differing on which entity was the rightful "China"—the PRC or the ROC. Chiang Kai-shek did not allow the United States to pursue a more creative approach that would have attempted to secure representation in international organizations for both the PRC and Taiwan.[27] Although this position was not unanimous among Taiwan's population, its citizens could not express their views under Chiang's authoritarian rule. Given the Taiwan government's position, however, it did not pursue independence or otherwise challenge the status quo.

Despite holding starkly different views on Taiwan's status, for decades China, Taiwan, and the United States refrained from seeking to fundamentally overturn the status quo and did not cross each other's red lines. The United States has maintained only unofficial relations with Taiwan, as establishing formal diplomatic relations with the island would necessitate severing relations with Beijing. China, while increasing its coercion of Taiwan, has not set a formal deadline for unification or pressured Taiwan to enter political negotiations. Although Taiwan's Democratic Progressive Party (DPP), which has traditionally advocated for independence, pushed the envelope when it pursued a referendum in 2008 on joining the United Nations under the name "Taiwan," it has since moderated its stance, asserting that Taiwan does not need to declare independence because it is already an independent country, the "Republic of China (Taiwan)."

With this political framework and China's economic liberalization as a foundation, cross-strait economic ties boomed, with Taiwanese investment helping fuel the PRC's economic rise and Taiwanese businesses benefiting from the PRC's low labor costs.[28] During the three decades between 1991 and 2021, Taiwanese investment in the PRC totaled $194 billion.[29] Cross-strait trade exploded, rising from $342 million in 1990 to $208 billion in 2021.[30] China is now Taiwan's largest trading partner, accounting for nearly 23 percent of its foreign trade, a number that increases to 30 percent if Hong Kong is included. With the help of this two-way trade, Taiwan's gross domestic product (GDP) grew from $166 billion in 1990 to $775 billion in 2021.[31]

The status quo is under increasing strain as China, Taiwan, and the United States reevaluate whether the long-standing political formulation continues to serve their respective interests.

A number of factors—the emergence of a stronger and more assertive China, the rise of a distinct Taiwanese identity and the Taiwanese people's lack of interest in becoming part of the PRC, growing U.S. support for Taiwan, and the steady deterioration of U.S.-China relations—have combined to prompt Beijing, Taipei, and Washington to question both the desirability of the status quo and one another's commitment to it.

The Chinese government believes that Taiwan's separation was an injustice that the country had to endure because of its previous weakness. Its 2022 white paper on Taiwan reflected, "from the mid-19th century, due to the aggression of Western powers and the decadence of feudal rule, China…went through a period of suffering worse than anything it had previously known…Japan's 50-year occupation of Taiwan epitomized this humiliation…The fact that we have not yet been reunified is a scar left by history on the Chinese nation."[32]

In the eyes of China's leaders, the country no longer needs to tolerate what it was forced to when it was weak. Xi is using China's growing power to alter the status quo, turning to coercive tools, such as military threats, diplomatic pressure, economic sanctions, and disinformation campaigns to erode public confidence in U.S. support, undermine Taiwan's elected government, and convince Taiwanese people that unification with—and submission to—China is inevitable and therefore resistance is dangerous and ultimately futile. Beijing is also using economic leverage and information operations to try to build support or at least tolerance in Taiwan for a process leading to unification. China's strategy is less risky than using force and is difficult for Taiwan or the United States to counter, but at the same time, it has largely backfired by increasing the sense of Taiwanese identity and further alienating the Taiwanese public from the PRC.

Taiwan's development into a vibrant democracy has allowed its citizens to express their opinions on cross-strait relations, while China's turn toward even greater authoritarianism has made the Taiwanese more skeptical of living under PRC rule. Chiang Kai-shek, like his PRC counterparts, endorsed a "One China" framework, agreeing that Taiwan and the mainland were both a part of the same polity but asserting that the Republic of China was the rightful government of all of China. For over four decades, this was the only view that could be publicly held in Taiwan. During the period of martial law that lasted until 1987, the KMT could theoretically have concluded a deal with Beijing and imposed its decision on the population. With Taiwan's democratization in the 1980s and 1990s, however, citizens could challenge the KMT's narrative and express a separate Taiwanese identity. As a result, most Taiwanese do not view their political status as in any way linked to the Chinese Civil War and do not want unification. Instead, they would point to the separate national and political identity that they have forged over decades as evidence that Taiwan should be viewed on its own terms and recognized as a separate polity. China's crackdown on democracy and civil society in Hong Kong has accelerated these trends, convincing many Taiwanese that they cannot trust PRC promises and leading them to reject unification in any form. Another result of Taiwan's democratization is that any change in the relationship between Taiwan and China now requires a constitutional amendment, which must be approved by three-fourths of the members of Taiwan's legislature and a majority of all eligible voters.

Reflecting these changing views within Taiwan, the share of Taiwanese people who favor moving toward unification has dropped significantly over time, while support for independence has dramatically risen (see figure 3).[33] These polls likely underestimate popular support for independence; a different survey found that more than two-thirds of Taiwanese support independence if Taiwan could still maintain peaceful relations with the PRC.[34] This shift is occurring despite a continued affinity among Taiwanese people for Chinese culture and ultimately is rooted in a rejection of the PRC's political system.[35]

In the United States, Taiwan's evolution into a democracy and a growing appreciation for its strategic importance, paired with increasing PRC pressure on Taiwan, have increased calls to upgrade relations and visibly demonstrate support for Taiwan. U.S.-Taiwan relations have consistently evolved to include more high-level interactions, but they are entering a qualitatively new territory. In 2020, for instance, the Trump administration lifted many "self-imposed restrictions" on contact with Taipei's representatives in Washington, which the Biden administration upheld.[36] Two former senior officials in the Trump administration, after stepping down, also called for the United States to abandon its One China policy and recognize Taiwan as an independent country.[37] In 2021, two Republican congressmen introduced a bill advocating that the United States walk away from its One China policy and recognize Taiwan as an independent country; the bill was reintroduced in 2023 with eighteen Republican cosponsors.[38]

Those calling for the United States to recognize Taiwan as an independent country are decidedly in the minority, as doing so would lead to a rupture in U.S.-China relations and could prompt major Chinese military action against Taiwan. In addition, if China were to take such an action following this unilateral U.S. move, it would be far more difficult for the United States to bring together an international coalition to sanction China or to enlist the help of regional allies for a defense of Taiwan. Instead, the United States would be cast as a destabilizing force, and the Taiwanese people would pay the greatest cost. Thus U.S.

Figure 3

Few Taiwanese Desire Unification, With the Majority Preferring to Maintain the Status Quo

Public opinion polling of residents of Taiwan

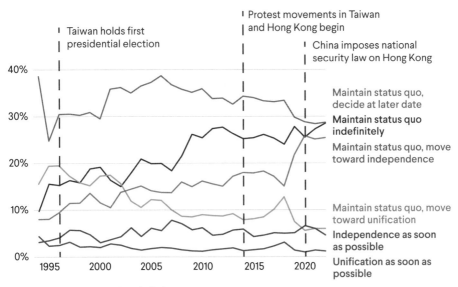

Note: Non-responses are excluded.

Source: Election Study Center, National Chengchi University.

recognition of Taiwan as an independent country would be irresponsible and ill-advised. At the same time, however, growing calls for such a change in U.S. policy have put more pressure on presidential administrations to demonstrate support for Taiwan.

Objecting to steps the United States has taken regarding relations with Taiwan, China has accused the United States of having a "fake" One China policy.[39] The United States asserts that its actions are consistent with its One China policy and are a necessary response to heightened Chinese coercion of Taiwan. This discord has created an action-reaction dynamic whereby China puts pressure on Taiwan, prompting the United States to take steps to demonstrate its support for Taiwan, in turn leading to more Chinese pressure on the island.

The Chinese government has also accused Taiwanese President Tsai Ing-wen of covertly pursuing independence by changing history textbooks to emphasize elements of Taiwan's history that do not center on its relationship to China, redesigning passports to display "Republic of China" in a smaller typeface to give prominence to the name "Taiwan," and further pursuing "de-Sinicization."[40] To show its displeasure, China has shut off all channels of communication with Taiwan's government, expanded disinformation and influence operations targeting the island, increased military activities near Taiwan—including erasing the median line in the Taiwan Strait—and ratcheted up economic pressure.

Each side is now accusing the other of altering the status quo, while perceiving its own actions as necessary defensive steps to prevent further erosion of the status quo. The United States believes that its moves to strengthen ties with Taiwan are necessary responses to PRC provocations and that cross-strait relations are more stable when Taiwan can approach the PRC from a position of self-confidence and strength. China is convinced that the United States has effectively abandoned its One China policy, that it is actively endorsing or implicitly emboldening an independence movement in Taiwan, and that U.S. support for Taiwan remains the primary obstacle standing between China and its ability to achieve unification. In Taiwan's democratic system, where leaders have to appeal to the voters who are alarmed by the PRC's coercive actions, there is little desire for more cross-strait integration or political negotiations that would lead to PRC control, and there is growing impatience with Taiwan's lack of international recognition.

As a result of these dynamics, reassurances offered by each side over the past seven years are deemed by the other parties to be either insincere or inadequate. Despite Washington's public and private statements that it continues to adhere to its One China policy and does not support Taiwan's independence, Beijing believes that its actions belie those words and that Washington is using Taiwan to contain China.[41] Though the Chinese government continues to publicly assert that it prefers to achieve peaceful unification, its coercive actions toward Taiwan and continued focus on developing a viable military option to capture the island leave the United States and Taiwan questioning its intentions. China's failure to abide by its commitments to Hong Kong or to honor its pledges to the United States not to militarize the South China Sea or conduct cyber espionage for commercial gain have led many in Taipei and Washington to doubt whether any reassurances Beijing offers can be trusted.

For decades, analysts have assessed that China is willing to defer using force against Taiwan as long as it believes it can achieve peaceful unification at some point in the future. Because of the recent change in dynamics between Taiwan and China, however, the prospect of a peaceful and consensual resolution of cross-strait differences has grown increasingly remote. The PRC is likely to conclude that if it wants to achieve unification, it will need to resort to nonpeaceful means to do so.

The most consequential change to cross-strait dynamics has been Taiwan's democratization and the emergence of a separate political identity. According to one long-running poll, whereas only 18 percent of those in Taiwan identified as "Taiwanese" in 1992 (the first year of the survey), now nearly 64 percent identify as such, while those who identify as "Chinese" has declined from 25.5 percent to 2.4 percent and those who identify as "both Taiwanese and Chinese" has declined from 46 percent to 30 percent (see figure 4).[42] Accompanying this rise in Taiwanese identity has been a steep decline in support for unification and increased support for independence (see figure 3).

Taiwan's growing alienation from China is driven above all by the PRC's turn toward even greater authoritarianism and its violation of "One Country, Two Systems" in Hong Kong, which remains its proposed model for Taiwan. Under that arrangement, which Deng Xiaoping first introduced in the 1980s, the ROC would cease to exist, the PRC would govern Taiwan as a "special administrative region," and it would control the island's foreign and defense affairs. Taiwan would be allowed to maintain a separate economic and social system, and it would be granted a "high degree of autonomy" to oversee its internal affairs, but Beijing would be able to exercise a veto over Taipei's leaders.

In recent years, however, Beijing has made clear that it has no intention of honoring the legally binding commitments that it made when it took possession of Hong Kong, which has had chilling effects in Taiwan. In 2019, after Hong Kong's government put forth a bill that would allow individuals from Hong Kong to be extradited to the PRC, massive protests erupted, which police quelled using tear gas and rubber bullets. Although Hong Kong's government eventually withdrew the bill, China imposed a "national security law" the following year that severely curtails the rights of Hong Kong residents by targeting crimes of "secession" and "subversion." The authorities have arrested protestors, former opposition lawmakers, and journalists under the auspices

Figure 4

Taiwanese Identity Has Increased Over Time
Public opinion polling of residents of Taiwan

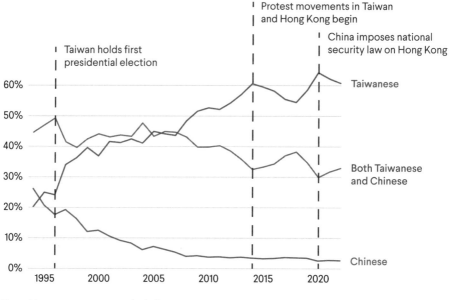

Note: Non-responses are excluded.

Source: Election Study Center, National Chengchi University.

of this and earlier laws, demonstrating the meaninglessness of China's pledges that Hong Kong would "enjoy a high degree of autonomy" and that its people would enjoy freedom of speech, of the press, and of assembly.[43]

As these events in Hong Kong were unfolding, Taiwanese concerns about unification increased dramatically. Rather than providing reassurances to Taiwan or putting forward another proposal for unification that would guarantee Taiwanese more rights and freedoms, China has moved in the opposite direction. The Chinese government insists that the implementation of One Country, Two Systems in Hong Kong is a "resounding success" and continues to view it as "the best approach to realizing national reunification" with Taiwan. Interestingly, however, Beijing has made clear that "One Country is the precondition and foundation of Two Systems; Two Systems is subordinate to and derives from One Country."[44] Presumably, this means that if protests were to occur in Taiwan following unification, the PRC would impose limits on the separate social systems, as it has done in Hong Kong.

The Chinese government has also reduced the number of guarantees it would offer to Taiwan under One Country, Two Systems, rendering an already unappealing proposal even more so. Whereas Beijing formerly pledged that the People's Liberation Army (PLA) would not have a presence in Taiwan and that Taiwan could maintain some semblance of a military, in a major speech in 2019 Xi did not provide this reassurance. Xi also did not guarantee that Taiwan would be allowed to maintain its political institutions following unification. Instead, he pledged that "the social system and lifestyles of Taiwan compatriots will be fully respected...and the private property, religious beliefs, and legitimate rights and interests of Taiwan compatriots will be fully guaranteed."[45] Beijing, however, could be expected to define "legitimate rights and interests" narrowly, to exclude most political rights.

Regardless of the specific offer Beijing makes to Taipei, its pledges will not be taken seriously given its actions in Hong Kong. Despite the Sino-British Joint Declaration's status as a recognized international treaty, China's foreign ministry spokesman explicitly dismissed it as a "historical document" that "no longer has any practical significance, and it is not at all binding for the central government's management over Hong Kong."[46] As long as China continues to put forward One Country, Two Systems as the only basis for peaceful unification and flouts this arrangement in Hong Kong, the likelihood of peacefully resolving cross-strait differences is remote.

As the prospect of achieving peaceful unification grows more remote, China will increasingly employ coercive tools against Taiwan.

China is already using a range of tools against Taiwan to achieve its political objectives, including military threats, diplomatic pressure, economic sanctions, information campaigns, and psychological operations (see figure 5). Although Beijing continues to develop its military options for Taiwan contingencies—which could take the form of a quarantine or blockade of the island, missile strikes against critical infrastructure, the seizure of one or more of Taiwan's offshore islands, or a full invasion—the risk that these options carry means it likely views force as the last resort. Instead, the PRC will presumably attempt to gain control of Taiwan by leveraging an array of coercive instruments. Although the PRC views coercion as being consistent with peaceful unification, Taiwan and the United States would argue that relying on such pressure is incompatible with a consensual resolution of cross-strait issues. Nonetheless, in the years ahead, this pressure will likely intensify and could enter a qualitatively new realm.

Beijing's preferred course of action is to take a series of diplomatic, economic, military, and covert steps that taken alone do not rise to the level of prompting an international response but together could cause the Taiwanese people to lose faith in their ability to resist and doubt that countries will assist them. The Chinese government's hope is that this prompts the Taiwanese public to support political leaders who favor negotiated acquiescence to its political demands.

On the diplomatic front, China is attempting to peel away the roughly dozen remaining countries that maintain diplomatic relations with Taiwan by offering them economic inducements to instead establish diplomatic ties with the PRC. These relationships are important to Taiwan for a number of reasons; these countries often advocate for Taiwan's participation in international organizations, and formal diplomatic ties with countries provide a psychological boost to the Taiwanese people. During President Tsai's administration, to signal its displeasure that she did not explicitly endorse the 1992 Consensus (a formulation whereby Taiwan agrees that there is one China in the world but asserts that there are different interpretations as to which government is the rightful representative of China), the PRC has persuaded nine countries—Burkina Faso, the Dominican Republic, El Salvador, Honduras, Kiribati, Nicaragua, Panama, Sao Tome and Principe, and the Solomon Islands—to sever diplomatic relations with Taiwan. Beijing also pressures countries to narrow their unofficial relations with Taiwan, which is an even more worrisome development because Taiwan's most important relationships are with countries that do not formally recognize it.

China is also blocking Taiwan's participation in the world's leading international organizations, which require that members be sovereign states recognized as such by their peers. Without UN membership, Taiwan can only participate in meetings within the UN system when China allows it to do so, and China uses this leverage as a bargaining chip. For instance, after Taiwanese President Ma Ying-jeou endorsed the 1992 Consensus, China allowed Taiwan to participate in meetings of the World Health Assembly from 2009 to 2016 under the name "Chinese Taipei." In 2013, China allowed Taiwan to attend the International Civil Aviation Organization (ICAO) assembly as a "special guest" of the president of the ICAO Council. When President Tsai declined to endorse the 1992 Consensus, China intervened to ensure that Taiwan

Figure 5

China's Coercion of Taiwan Is Vast and Persistent

Coercive actions during the presidency of Tsai Ing-wen, as of April 2023

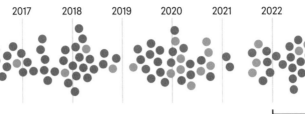

| | 2017 | 2018 | 2019 | 2020 | 2021 | 2022 | 2023 |

● Political and diplomatic
● Economic
● Military*
● Psychological

*Orange dots indicate the first instance of a military action which in many cases is repeated. Subsequent instances of the same action are not included.

Shown below

Steps taken since January 2022:

Political and diplomatic

After Chinese pressure, Taiwan unable to join WHO assembly

Taiwanese visitors to the World Cup forced to enter Qatar under the name "Chinese Taipei"

China imposes visa bans on Taiwanese political figures

China threatens Lithuania amid closer Taiwan-Lithuania ties

Taiwan excluded from the International Civil Aviation Organization's 41st Assembly Session

Taiwan loses diplomatic ally Honduras to China

Economic

China bans grouper fish from Taiwan

China suspends natural sand exports to Taiwan hours after Pelosi lands in Taiwan

China bans thousands of Taiwanese food imports

China suspends some beer, liquor, and beverage imports from Taiwan

Military

China fires waves of missiles over the Taiwan Strait, including one that flies over Taiwan, and conducts extensive military drills near Taiwan

Chinese drones cross the Taiwan Strait median line for the first time

Following President Biden's signing of the NDAA that contained provisions on Taiwan, seventy-one Chinese aircraft are tracked around Taiwan, with forty-seven entering its air defense identification zone (ADIZ)

In response to President Tsai Ing-wen's meeting with Speaker of the House Kevin McCarthy, China conducts three days of intense military drills in the Taiwan Strait, which include simulating targeted strikes on Taiwan

Psychological

Taiwan's Investigation Bureau states China is using fake social media accounts to subvert the public's trust in government and meddle in elections

China launches disinformation campaign about Ukraine targeting Taiwan

China pays Taiwanese celebrities to conduct "cognitive warfare"

China asserts maritime sovereignty rights over the Taiwan Strait

Note: For the full list of coercive steps since 2016, see cfr.org/US-Taiwan.

Source: CFR research.

would not be allowed to participate in any such meetings. Today, Taiwanese passport holders cannot even visit the United Nations headquarters in New York as tourists due to PRC pressure.

In recent years, China's attempts to constrain Taiwan's international space have intensified. Chinese diplomats interrupted the proceedings of an international meeting on conflict diamonds (the Kimberly Process) in Australia until the hosts forced Taiwan's delegation to leave.[47] Chinese officials in Fiji disrupted Taiwan's national day reception by attempting to intimidate guests, and, after being confronted, physically assaulting a Taiwanese official.[48] China has also put pressure on multinational companies to alter their websites so that Taiwan is not displayed as a country in drop-down menus.

China has already employed economic coercion against Taiwan and could both expand the scope of such pressure and use it to influence domestic politics in Taiwan. After President Tsai came into office, China placed limits on tourism to Taiwan. In 2021, China banned the import of Taiwanese pineapples (90 percent of Taiwan's pineapple exports went to China), and subsequently banned Taiwanese wax and sugar apples, grouper, and meat.[49] Beijing's most significant moves to date followed U.S. Speaker of the House Nancy Pelosi's visit to Taiwan, after which it announced import bans on more than two thousand Taiwanese agricultural products and introduced an export ban on natural sand to Taiwan (a critical input to the manufacture of semiconductors).[50] China has also pressured Taiwanese companies operating in the PRC to publicly voice support for the 1992 Consensus and oppose Taiwan independence.[51] And China typically targets industries and regions in Taiwan that support the DPP in an attempt to harm the party's electoral chances.

China has also regularized military activity in the Taiwan Strait and established a new baseline for its operations. This shift is most starkly visible in the PLA's near-daily flights through Taiwan's self-declared air defense identification zone (ADIZ); in 2022, Chinese military aircraft entered this airspace on 268 of 365 days (see figure 6). In addition to increasing the frequency of these flights, the PLA has increased their sophistication, including its most advanced fighter jets, nuclear-capable bombers, and early warning aircraft in the patrols. In addition, following Pelosi's visit to Taiwan, the PLA effectively erased the median line in the Taiwan Strait, an important demarcation that helped the two sides avoid incidents by operating across that line. During that same period, the PLA fired ballistic missiles around Taiwan (including at least one that flew over the island), operated near Taiwan's territorial seas, and

Figure 6

Chinese Military Planes Are Entering Taiwan's ADIZ With Increasing Frequency

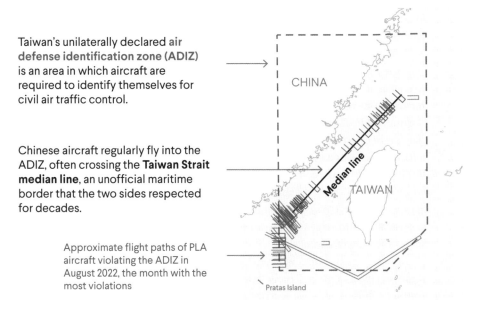

Taiwan's unilaterally declared **air defense identification zone (ADIZ)** is an area in which aircraft are required to identify themselves for civil air traffic control.

Chinese aircraft regularly fly into the ADIZ, often crossing the **Taiwan Strait median line**, an unofficial maritime border that the two sides respected for decades.

Approximate flight paths of PLA aircraft violating the ADIZ in August 2022, the month with the most violations

Chinese aircraft violating Taiwan's ADIZ by month

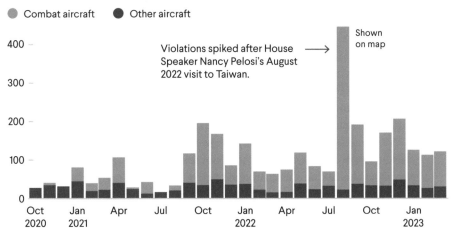

Notes: Flight paths shown on the map include multiple aircraft. While Taiwan's ADIZ extends to cover a portion of the PRC, its Ministry of National Defense only tracks PLA aircraft that enter the ADIZ east of the Taiwan Strait median line.

Source: Taiwan Ministry of National Defense, data compiled by Gerald Brown and Ben Lewis.

established a presence of naval vessels closer to Taiwan. These actions have real operational consequences, allowing the PLA to conduct exercises for Taiwan contingencies and test the readiness of Taiwan's military, shrink the warning time that would be available if it chose to initiate hostilities, and potentially disguise the opening salvo of a conflict as a routine exercise.

China will look to increase the scope and intensity of its coercive activities aimed at Taiwan. The South China Sea offers an instructive case study and demonstrates that China will seek to take piecemeal actions that cannot be reversed to create a new baseline or "new normal." These "gray zone" tactics are especially effective against Taiwan because its leaders have fewer options to respond and cannot afford to be seen as escalating cross-strait tensions or causing a crisis; Beijing is able to exploit this asymmetry and act without fear of losing control of escalatory dynamics. In addition, because any one of these actions, taken in isolation, does not pose an existential threat to Taiwan, it is far more difficult for the United States to respond without being seen as fueling tensions.

One area that China is likely to turn to, with the South China Sea again serving as a precedent, is "lawfare," or the use of law as a weapon of conflict. China could choose to unilaterally declare that it will not respect Taiwan's territorial waters or airspace or that it will administer Taiwan's waters and airspace because, in its view, Taiwan is a part of China and the PRC is the sole legal government of China. It could follow this announcement by sailing ships within twelve nautical miles of Taiwan's coast and even flying military aircraft over the island of Taiwan. Doing so would force Taiwan's military to either ignore a blatant violation of its sovereignty, which would deal a significant blow to the Taiwanese government's credibility, or to fire the first shot and risk being seen as the initiator of a conflict. Particularly worrisome is a scenario in which Beijing requires civilian aircraft and cargo vessels heading for Taiwan to submit to PRC aviation and customs control on the grounds that the PRC has jurisdiction over the waters and airspace surrounding Taiwan. There is already evidence that the PRC could be contemplating such an action: following President Tsai's meeting with U.S. Speaker of the House Kevin McCarthy in California in April 2023, the PRC announced an inspection operation in the Taiwan Strait and reserved the right to board cargo ships. Though it appears that China did not actually board any ship, this could be the first step in testing such a tactic.[52]

The chance of a conflict will rise as Xi Jinping approaches the end of his tenure and the basis of his legitimacy shifts from delivering economic growth to satisfying Chinese nationalism.

The biggest question going forward is what Xi Jinping's intentions are vis-à-vis Taiwan and how important he deems the subjugation of Taiwan for his legacy. Although he has not put an explicit timeline on achieving unification with Taiwan and continues to assert a preference for peaceful unification (while keeping open the option to use military force), indicators suggest that he could seek to resolve this issue on his watch.

Xi has repeatedly linked unification with Taiwan to the "rejuvenation of the Chinese nation," which he has stated must be achieved by 2049.[53] Beijing's 2022 white paper on Taiwan asserts that achieving unification "is indispensable" and "an essential step" for achieving China's rejuvenation. The paper continues, "The Taiwan question arose as a result of weakness and chaos in our nation, and it will be resolved as national rejuvenation becomes a reality."[54] Xi's subsequent report to the Twentieth National Congress of the Communist Party of China notes, "Resolving the Taiwan question and realizing China's complete reunification is…a natural requirement for realizing the rejuvenation of the Chinese nation."[55] Xi went even further in his March 2023 speech to the National People's Congress, asserting that achieving unification "is the essence of national rejuvenation."[56] Although Xi is not the first Chinese leader to tie unification with rejuvenation, he is linking the two more explicitly than any of his predecessors.

Taken at face value, an implicit timeline of 2049 would give the United States ample time to reinforce deterrence and prepare for a potential conflict in the Taiwan Strait, with the goal of heading one off. It would also provide the opportunity for a successor to Xi to emerge who might not be as wedded to this timeline. Given that Xi most likely will not be ruling China in 2049 (he would be ninety-six years old), the question turns to whether he is determined to resolve this on his watch and is working under a tighter timeline. Xi has stated that the Taiwan issue "cannot be passed from generation to generation," which could mean that he will not hand this off to his successor.[57] Xi clearly sees himself as a pivotal leader who should go down in history on par with Mao Zedong. It is unclear, however, what he would point to as his achievements to justify such a claim. Taking Taiwan, something that eluded Mao and Deng, would cement his place in history. Thus, there is a possibility that Xi is growing impatient with the status quo and believes that Taiwan is central to his legacy. That said, windows into Xi's thinking are far from clear.

Senior U.S. officials have echoed this line of analysis, indicating that they believe Xi could be determined to bring Taiwan under the PRC's control in an abbreviated timeline. CIA Director William Burns stated in July 2022 that he "wouldn't underestimate…Xi's determination to assert China's control" over Taiwan and that "the risks of that become higher…the further into this decade that you get."[58] Director of National Intelligence Avril Haines assessed that the threat to Taiwan "is critical or acute between now and 2030."[59] Secretary of State Antony Blinken stated, "What's changed is this: the decision by the government in Beijing that that status quo is no longer acceptable, that they wanted to speed up the process by which they would pursue reunification."[60] Finally, Admiral John Aquilino, commander of U.S. Indo-Pacific Command (INDOPACOM), noted, "I see actions that give me concern that the timeline is shrinking" and that "this problem is much closer to us than most think."[61] Such assessments could suggest that Xi is focused on achieving progress on Taiwan to mark the hundredth anniversary of the establishment of the PLA or the end of his third term (2027) or fourth term (2032).

Beyond a desire to build his legacy, Xi could also be driven by the need to rebuild the foundation for the CCP's political legitimacy.

Beyond a desire to build his legacy, Xi could also be driven by the need to rebuild the foundation for the CCP's political legitimacy. For over four decades, the CCP has enjoyed an implicit social contract with the Chinese people whereby it delivers sustained economic growth and, in exchange, its monopoly on power is not challenged. China's economy has not contracted since Deng Xiaoping ushered in the period of "reform and opening" in late 1978, with its economy expanding by an average of more than 9 percent annually from 1980 to 2021. Over that period, China's annual GDP has increased nearly fifty-fold, from $300 billion to $14.9 trillion.[62] But China is now confronted with an array of issues, above all an aging and shrinking population and slowing productivity growth. Investing in infrastructure and the property sector, the CCP's favored tool to prop up economic growth, has run its course. Xi's policies—principally his turn toward statism, his crackdown on innovative technology companies, his embrace of a zero-COVID policy for three years, his failure to implement much-needed economic reforms, and his assertive foreign policy that has prompted countries to rethink economic ties—have also contributed to China's economic challenges.[63] U.S. policies, above all export controls on advanced technologies, will also make it harder for China to achieve sustained growth. As a result, China is likely entering a long-term economic slowdown.

As China's economic growth has slowed under Xi, he has increasingly turned to nationalism to justify the CCP's monopoly on power. With a further downturn, he could turn to the Taiwan issue to rally support for the CCP and his personal rule. As Xi approaches the end of his tenure and looks toward his legacy, the risk of a conflict over Taiwan will grow.

Economics

Taiwan's critical role in global supply chains—above all semiconductor production—acts as a brake to hostilities but does not diminish China's desire to gain control over Taiwan.

It is difficult to overstate the critical role that Taiwan plays in the global semiconductor market. Taiwanese companies hold a 68 percent market share in the manufacture of semiconductors (see figure 7). Taiwan Semiconductor Manufacturing Company (TSMC) is the world's largest contract chipmaker and produces around 90 percent of the world's leading-edge semiconductors.[64] No other company can produce chips at scale as sophisticated as the ones TSMC manufactures. These chips provide the computing power for everything from smartphones to weapons and cars, many of which require thousands of chips to function, and form the foundation of military, economic, and geopolitical power.[65]

China is highly reliant on chips manufactured in Taiwan, to manufacture products both for export (e.g., iPhones) and for its domestic market. In 2022, China imported $415 billion worth of semiconductors, exceeding its imports of oil.[66] China has sought to reduce its reliance on imported semiconductors by building a domestic supply chain and developing globally competitive national semiconductor champions. In 2014, it established a $23 billion Integrated Circuit Industry Investment Fund (also known as the Big Fund). Various subnational governments then created additional sister funds that invested in domestic semiconductor firms, including a $32 billion fund established by the Beijing municipal government.[67] The following year, China unveiled *Made in China 2025*, an ambitious industrial policy that explicitly set a target of reaching 40 percent self-sufficiency in chips by 2020 and 70 percent by

Figure 7

Led by TSMC, Taiwanese Companies Dominate the Global Semiconductor Market

Market share of semiconductor foundries, 2021

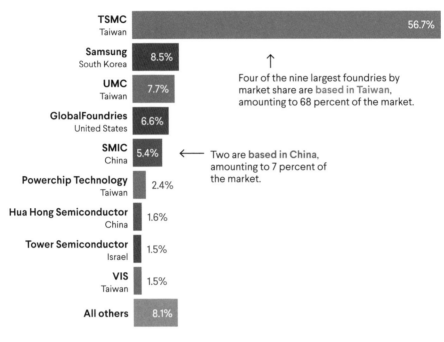

Source: CFR research.

2025. As China plowed money into developing semiconductor expertise, its two largest state-owned semiconductor firms, Tsinghua Unigroup and Semiconductor Manufacturing International Corporation (SMIC), received government support equivalent to more than 30 percent of their annual revenue.[68]

These efforts have thus far borne little fruit, and China has failed to produce a serious rival to TSMC. Far from reaching its goal of 70 percent self-sufficiency, China reportedly has a self-sufficiency in semiconductors that is closer to 16 percent.[69] Reports of serious corruption in China's Big Fund have surfaced.[70] Tsinghua Unigroup and SMIC, plagued by inefficiencies and high debt, have made limited progress. Further, they are led by former TSMC executives, which demonstrates Beijing's continued reliance on Taiwanese expertise.[71]

China's dependence on imported chips is a major vulnerability, one exacerbated by U.S. export controls imposed in 2022 that place severe restrictions on the ability of companies (both U.S. and foreign) to sell both advanced chips and the equipment used to manufacture them to China and that bar U.S. persons from providing services to China's semiconductor firms.[72] Despite their best efforts, PRC semiconductor firms remain wholly reliant on foreign technology and equipment, which are almost entirely produced by the United States or its close allies and are covered by these restrictions.

President Tsai, among others, has referred to Taiwan's dominance of the semiconductor manufacturing industry as a "silicon shield" that deters China from invading the island.[73] Like-minded analysts argue that China is so dependent on Taiwanese chips that it cannot afford a war that would destroy these foundries or render them inoperable, because such an outcome would devastate China's economy. China's interest in ensuring that unification can occur at some point in the future, however, trumps such economic considerations. Thus, if Taiwan were to formally declare independence, China would almost certainly attack regardless of the economic fallout, having accepted the enormous cost of an attack.

Some take the opposite stance, arguing that Taiwan's dominance of semiconductor manufacturing makes a Chinese assault more likely because if China seizes these foundries, it could immediately solve its domestic chip production problem and even turn this tool against countries like the United States. China's desire to achieve unification with Taiwan, however, predates the semiconductor industry and should not be ascribed to the latter's semiconductor prowess. In addition, even if China seized Taiwan, it would be wholly incapable of operating Taiwan's fabrication facilities (or "fabs" in industry speak). These factories require deep operational expertise, and Taiwan's engineers would almost certainly flee during a conflict or refuse to work for future Chinese owners. The facilities also need continued access to U.S. and allied technologies and equipment to function, and the United States would presumably refuse to provide any support if China were to gain control over Taiwan.

The extent to which Taiwan, China, and the United States are integrated through global supply chains and rely on one another for critical inputs in part deters all three parties from acting irresponsibly and gives each a stake in preserving the status quo. At the same time, political considerations will trump economic ones if a Chinese leader believes that peaceful unification is irreversibly drifting out of reach. If Xi or his successor reaches that conclusion and believes that a military operation can succeed, they will likely order the use of force regardless of the dire economic consequences. At the same time, a Chinese leader is unlikely to order an invasion out of the fanciful assumption that doing so is an easy way to solve China's inability to produce advanced chips.

In addition to the devastation for the people of Taiwan, a conflict would also trigger a global economic depression and an open-ended era of hostility between the world's two leading powers.

Any conflict over Taiwan would devastate the global economy by closing off vital shipping lanes, halting the production and delivery of semiconductors, and likely stopping trade between China and the West. According to one study, a Chinese blockade of Taiwan would cause $2.5 trillion in annual global economic losses by bringing countless supply chains to a halt and forcing them to try to move forward without Taiwanese components.[74]

Almost every electronic device contains chips, many of which are made in Taiwan (see figure 8). Losing access to these chips would cause global production of smartphones to be at least halved, and the manufacture of everything from computers to cars, weapons, and microwaves would be severely constrained. Many of the biggest U.S. companies, from Apple to General Motors, would struggle to produce anything. Replacing lost Taiwanese capacity would take years.

Taiwan's location astride major shipping arteries, principally the South China Sea and East China Sea, would force trade in the region to a standstill while a blockade or attack was ongoing. A conflict over Taiwan would also dramatically increase insurance premiums and shipping costs for commercial carriers and producers. In 2016, the UN Conference on Trade and Development (UNCTAD) estimated that roughly 80 percent of global trade by volume and 70 percent by value is transported by sea. Of that maritime trade, 60 percent passes through Asia, with the South China Sea carrying an estimated one-third of global shipping.[75] Another study estimated that $3.4 trillion in trade passed through the South China Sea in 2016; despite significant disruptions to maritime activity associated with COVID-19 between 2020 and 2022, these numbers are still roughly accurate today.[76] Approximately 48 percent of the world's 5,400 operational container ships and 88 percent of the world's largest ships by tonnage passed through the Taiwan Strait in 2022.[77] Most, if not all, of these commercial ships would have to find alternate routes during a conflict, stressing and potentially even

Figure 8

Semiconductors Enable Modern Life and Are Critical to Economies

Semiconductor demand by end use, 2021

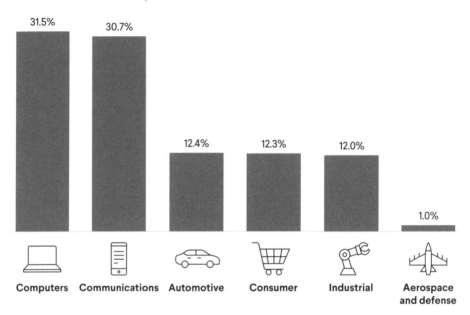

Source: Semiconductor Industry Association.

breaking global supply chains, with huge ramifications for companies and consumers alike.

During a conflict in the Taiwan Strait, the United States would presumably heavily sanction China and halt most trade with it, whether or not it decides to intervene militarily on Taiwan's behalf. U.S.-China trade in goods in 2022 reached a record high of nearly $700 billion, with the United States importing $537 billion of Chinese products.[78] As the COVID-19 pandemic revealed, many goods produced in China, in this case personal protective equipment, are difficult to source at scale from other countries. If China were to attack Taiwan, the rupture of U.S.-China trade relations would also severely hurt U.S. businesses and consumers.

While there is a lively debate on whether the United States and China are already locked in a cold war, a hot war over Taiwan would set off open-ended hostility between the two largest economies in the world and two nuclear-armed powers. It is virtually impossible to imagine Washington and Beijing working together in a meaningful way to address global issues such as public health, climate change, or nonproliferation either during or after a war over Taiwan. In addition, although countries throughout the world do not want to choose between the United States and China, a direct clash between the two countries would increase pressure on third countries to take sides, likely locking in opposing blocs for years or decades. The world after a war between the United States and China would be far poorer, more insecure, and less able to contend with global challenges.

Taiwan's dependence on trade with China provides Beijing with leverage over Taipei that could reduce the latter's options during a crisis.

Taiwan is highly reliant on international trade to generate economic growth, with trade equaling roughly 103 percent of its annual (nominal) GDP.[79] China, as Taiwan's largest trading partner, is the biggest contributor to Taiwan's GDP. Semiconductors accounted for 62 percent of the island's exports to China in 2021, with the total value of those sales reaching $155 billion. In the first half of 2022, China imported $79 billion worth of chips from Taiwan.[80] In addition to semiconductors, major Taiwanese exports to China include machinery, plastics, rubbers, and chemical products.

Beijing could intensify its economic pressure on Taipei to extract concessions or force it to enter political negotiations. If this were to happen, Taiwan would have to choose between its continued autonomy and its economic livelihood, a reality that provides China with leverage over Taiwan. To be sure, a Chinese decision to significantly cut trade with Taiwan would also deal a devastating blow to its own economy given its reliance on Taiwanese semiconductors, but Beijing can presumably afford to be less responsive to its citizens than Taipei.

China has already employed economic coercion against countries around the world, including Australia, Japan, Lithuania, Norway, and the Philippines, as well as Taiwan. This has included limiting Chinese tourism to Taiwan, increasing port inspections of Taiwanese goods, banning some Taiwanese agricultural and food products, and halting the export of natural sand to Taiwan. China has also pressured Taiwanese companies operating in the PRC to publicly support the 1992 Consensus and oppose Taiwanese independence, in essence asserting that as a precondition of their ability to do business in China.

At the same time, China has refrained from employing its most powerful economic tools. Instead, it has pursued an economic strategy that has both carrots (incentivizing Taiwanese businesses to invest in the PRC) and sticks (punishing DPP supporters). In doing so, China is seeking to influence Taiwan's political trajectory by promoting pro-China voices and creating divisions within Taiwan. Thus, even though cross-strait relations have deteriorated since 2016, China has not suspended any of its major economic agreements with Taiwan and has continued to introduce preferential policies for Taiwanese businesses.[81] As a result, China has left itself with plenty of levers that it could pull in the future to increase Taiwan's economic pain.

U.S. and allied reliance on semiconductors produced in Taiwan raises the stakes for the United States and the West in a conflict.

Although semiconductors were invented in the United States, the world's leading chips are designed domestically, and U.S. companies continue to produce specialized tools needed to manufacture semiconductors, the United States lacks the capacity to produce cutting-edge chips, and has seen market share across all types of chips decline substantially. U.S. fabs produced 37 percent of the world's chips in 1990, but this number fell by nearly two-thirds to 13 percent by 2010.[82] The United States relies on semiconductors produced in Taiwan (and to a far lesser extent South Korea) for roughly 90 percent of its supply of highly advanced logic chips.[83] Apple's most advanced semiconductors, which contain billions of transistors, can only be produced in a single building within TSMC's sprawling campus in Taiwan.[84]

In addition to being integral to consumer electronics, chips also power every advanced weapon. U.S. Commerce Secretary Gina Raimondo, for instance, has noted that one Javelin anti-tank missile requires more than 250 chips and warned that at one point semiconductor shortages were hampering the ability of the United States to continue supplying weapons to Ukraine.[85] If China were to blockade Taiwan and cut off its international trade, companies that rely on semiconductors manufactured in Taiwan would have their annual revenue reduced by up to $1.6 trillion.[86] Many U.S. companies, including defense conglomerates, would need to dramatically dial back production, with serious consequences for U.S. economic and national security.

Recognizing this vulnerability, in 2022 Congress passed the CHIPS and Science Act, which provides $52 billion to jumpstart domestic semiconductor manufacturing, research and development, and workforce development.[87] Since 2020, more than three dozen U.S. companies, including industry giants Intel and Micron Technology, have pledged to invest nearly $200 billion in semiconductor manufacturing in the United States.[88] In addition, with significant U.S. encouragement, TSMC committed to building a semiconductor manufacturing facility in Arizona and later tripled its planned investment to $40 billion and added a second facility. As they become operational in 2024 and 2026, TSMC's Arizona facilities are projected to produce six hundred thousand wafers (the discs that chips are made on) annually, with an estimated end-product value of more than $40 billion.[89]

Even if this limited onshoring is successful, the United States will not become self-sufficient in semiconductor manufacturing for decades. TSMC has stated that it has no intention of moving research and development off Taiwan, and its plants in Arizona will need constant connections to Taiwan (e.g., engineers flying back and forth) to operate. Furthermore, TSMC has shown no desire to move its most advanced chipmaking capabilities from Taiwan. It is also unclear how the United States will replicate the ecosystem that Taiwan enjoys, principally hundreds of suppliers of critical inputs a short drive from TSMC's facilities. The United States will also need to undertake significant statutory, regulatory, and permitting reform if it wants to attract additional investments in semiconductor fabs and address its severe shortage of qualified engineers.[90] In short, much more domestic investment in advanced manufacturing capacity will be required to ensure long-run competitive advantages in the U.S. chip sector.[91] The United States will remain highly reliant on chips produced in Taiwan for the foreseeable future, which gives it a large stake in deterring a conflict over Taiwan.

U.S. and allied economic interdependence with China would complicate efforts to resist Chinese aggression against Taiwan and impose costs on Beijing.

A crucial lesson of the war in Ukraine is that economic interdependence does not prevent conflict and could in fact give the aggressor perceived leverage. Although some European leaders, most prominently former German Chancellor Angela Merkel, believed that close energy ties would restrain Russian President Vladimir Putin by tying Russian economic growth to continued peace in Europe, Putin weaponized this interdependence. Putin concluded that European countries would not impose heavy economic sanctions on Russia because doing so would inflict economic devastation on their economies. Though he miscalculated and European countries chose to impose sanctions at substantial economic cost to themselves, economic interdependence did not deter Putin and could have in fact contributed to his decision to go to war. In addition, while the United States and its European and Asian allies have sanctioned Russia, many countries have remained on the sidelines.

A similar dynamic could play out over Taiwan, with China calculating that countries are so dependent on access to its market and its manufacturing capacity that they would not impose meaningful sanctions if it invaded Taiwan. Indeed, U.S. allies in the Indo-Pacific such as Australia, Japan, and South Korea count China as their number one trading partner. Europe's largest economy, Germany, does as well. If a Chinese attack on Taiwan occurs while sanctions against Russia remain in place, countries could conclude that they cannot afford to sanction both China and Russia at the same time and absorb the economic consequences.

> If a Chinese attack on Taiwan occurs while sanctions against Russia remain in place, countries could conclude that they cannot afford to sanction both Russia and China at the same time and absorb the economic consequences.

China, however, is not leaving this to chance and is seeking to harden its economy to be less vulnerable to sanctions.[92] It is actively pursuing a strategy to make countries more economically reliant on China and to decrease its exposure to the global economy by indigenizing foreign technology and supply chains.[93] Recognizing that it is still vulnerable to technological bottlenecks, above all in semiconductors, China's most recent five-year plan stresses the need to achieve technological self-reliance and gives national security considerations equal weight as economic development.[94] The CCP's 2021 historical resolution touted its commitment to making "self-reliance in science and technology the strategic pillar for the country's development."[95]

Beyond these strategies and plans, China is taking tangible steps to "sanctions-proof" its economy. In 2020, China introduced an Export Control Law, which provides the basis for China to restrict exports on national security grounds.[96] The following year, China introduced an

Anti-Foreign Sanctions Law, which establishes a framework to punish foreign companies that comply with sanctions targeting China.[97] China presumably hopes that these laws will deter countries from sanctioning China by making clear that it could halt the export of critical commodities such as rare earth minerals in response to export controls placed in the wake of an invasion of Taiwan. China is also promoting use of the renminbi (RMB) for international transactions and trying to reduce its dependence on the U.S. dollar through currency swap agreements and other measures. Further, it is increasing its reserve of essential supplies, such as crude oil and food.

U.S. and allied economic interdependence with China (or, more accurately, dependence on China), paired with Chinese efforts to promote self-reliance, could prompt Xi to assess that sanctions would hurt the countries doing the sanctioning more than China. As a result, he could conclude that countries will be hesitant to levy draconian sanctions in response to Chinese aggression against Taiwan. If Chinese policies to promote indigenization and reduce reliance on foreign technology prove successful, the prospect of sanctions is less likely to influence Xi's calculus over time.

Security

In addition to having a legal obligation to maintain the capacity to defend Taiwan, the United States has vital strategic reasons for doing so.

A Chinese assault on Taiwan would gravely undermine an array of U.S. interests and weaken its position in the world's most economically consequential region. If China were to successfully annex Taiwan, such an outcome would also decisively shift the military balance of power in Asia in China's favor and make it far more difficult for the United States to defend its treaty allies or prevent a Chinese bid for regional hegemony.

Taiwan has inherent military value, and thus its fate will in large part determine the U.S. military's ability to operate in the region. As Assistant Secretary of Defense Ely Ratner noted, "Taiwan is located at a critical node within the first island chain, anchoring a network of U.S. allies and partners—stretching from the Japanese archipelago down to the Philippines and into the South China Sea—that is critical to the region's security and critical to the defense of vital U.S. interests in the Indo-Pacific" (see figure 9).[98] With Taiwan outside of its control and U.S. allies and partners arrayed throughout the first island chain, the PLA will struggle to project power far beyond China's shores. If China were to annex Taiwan and base military assets, such as underwater surveillance devices, submarines, and air defense units on the island, however, it would be able to limit the U.S. military's operations in the region and in turn its ability to defend its Asian allies.[99] U.S. policymakers should therefore understand that it is not only Taiwan's future at stake but also the future of the first island chain and the ability to preserve U.S. access and influence throughout the Western Pacific.

Figure 9

Taiwan's Location Along the First Island Chain Anchors a Network of U.S. Allies

What happens in the Taiwan Strait will also have enormous implications for the future of U.S. alliances in the region, which constitute the United States' most important asymmetric advantage vis-à-vis China. If the United States chose to stand aside in the face of Chinese aggression against Taiwan, U.S. allies would come to question whether they could rely on the United States. Having lost confidence in the U.S. commitment to their security, they would contemplate either accommodating China or hedging against it by growing their militaries or even developing nuclear weapons. Either outcome would result in diminished U.S. influence and increased global instability. The United States, for its part, would feel compelled to take steps to shore up its allies' confidence, which would likely result in riskier and costlier foreign policy decisions.

A Chinese attack on Taiwan, regardless of its success, would also trigger a global economic depression by halting production of the vast majority of the world's most advanced semiconductors. The United States would have to contend with a chip shortage that would force companies across a range of industries to reduce or even halt production. As mentioned, a Chinese blockade of Taiwan that halts all of Taiwan's international trade would cause $2.5 trillion in annual global economic losses, but this figure does not even take into account the second-order effects of possible sanctions, trade restrictions against China, the unavailability of equipment powered by Taiwanese chips that is critical for e-commerce, entertainment, and logistics, or the potential for military escalation.[100] These repercussions would be catastrophic and hard to reverse.

Politically, Taiwan is one of Asia's few democratic success stories and, according to one recent study, its freest society.[101] Taiwan's open political system demonstrates to PRC citizens that there is an alternative path of development for a majority ethnically Chinese society. As a result, Xi could well believe that Taiwan's very existence poses a threat to the CCP. If China were to annex Taiwan by force, its democracy would almost certainly be extinguished, and its twenty-three million people would see their rights severely curtailed. Such a development would shake democracies around the world.

Taiwan's fate also has important implications for international order, which have only been magnified by Russia's invasion of Ukraine. If China were to successfully absorb Taiwan in spite of Taiwanese resistance, it would establish a pattern of authoritarian countries using force to attack democratic neighbors and change borders. The most basic pillar of international relations—that countries cannot use force to alter borders—would be destroyed.

Deterrence is steadily eroding in the Taiwan Strait and is at risk of failing, increasing the likelihood of Chinese aggression.

For decades, the United States could assume that U.S. intervention on Taiwan's behalf would be decisive. U.S. arms provided Taiwan with a qualitative edge over the PLA, which lacked sophisticated weapons. As China prioritized economic development, military modernization took a back seat. The PLA was largely a ground-based force focused on China's land borders rather than an expeditionary military that could project power over the Taiwan Strait. Thus, during the 1995–96 Taiwan Strait Crisis, the United States sailed two aircraft carrier strike groups toward the Taiwan Strait as a show of force.

Largely driven by the Taiwan Strait Crisis, as well as the 1999 accidental U.S. bombing of the Chinese embassy in Belgrade, Serbia, China embarked on a comprehensive military modernization campaign, with the aim of developing capabilities that could deter and, if need be, defeat the United States in China's immediate periphery (often referred to as counter-intervention or anti-access/area-denial capabilities). For Beijing, Washington's intervention in Kosovo had direct bearing on Taiwan, as it demonstrated that the United States was willing to use military force absent a UN mandate to carve off a piece of a sovereign state.[102] Since then, preparing for a conflict in the Taiwan Strait has driven PLA force structure and procurement priorities.

China's official defense budget is now $225 billion, nearly doubling since 2013.[103] Even that remarkable growth, however, vastly understates the military capability that China has been able to build. China's published budget omits important categories such as research and development and foreign weapons purchases, and DOD estimates that its actual military-related spending could be up to two times higher than its reported budget.[104] Although U.S. defense spending outpaces China's, DOD has to spread its resources to prepare for a range of contingencies around the world, while China devotes the bulk of its resources to preparing for conflicts on its periphery, above all one over Taiwan. In addition, China's massive theft of U.S. defense–related intellectual property and dual-use technologies allows it to more cheaply develop new weapons.[105] As a result, China has developed an array of capabilities intended to win a war in the Taiwan Strait by delaying or denying U.S. intervention—principally ballistic missiles, submarines, modern air defense units stationed on China's east coast and reclaimed land in the South China Sea that can range beyond Taiwan, and advanced fighters and long-range bombers.

As a result of these sustained investments, the PLA Navy (PLAN) is now numerically the largest navy in the world (though the United States continues to exceed it by tonnage), with 340 ships and submarines, and is projected to add another 100 ships to its fleet by 2030. The PLA Air Force and PLAN Aviation together constitute the largest aviation force in the Indo-Pacific, with more than 2,800 total aircraft, and they are rapidly catching up to Western air forces in terms of capability, according to DOD.[106] The PLA has one thousand short-range ballistic missiles and six hundred medium-range ballistic missiles in its arsenal and is expected to use these missiles early in a conflict to destroy Taiwan's military bases and critical infrastructure.[107] The PLA is also improving its ability to undertake complex joint operations, conducting

Spotlight: Whither Strategic Ambiguity?

One element of U.S. policy that is increasingly debated is the approach known as strategic ambiguity. Under this policy, which is separate from the One China policy, the United States has chosen for decades not to explicitly state whether it would come to Taiwan's defense.[113] In essence, the United States has decided to keep both China and Taiwan guessing as to what it might do during a crisis, while reserving the option to come to Taiwan's direct defense. Those who support this stance argue that it allows the United States to simultaneously deter both PRC aggression, as Beijing surely assumes that Washington would intervene on Taiwan's behalf, as well as Taiwanese adventurism, as Taipei cannot be sure that Washington would intervene if it were seen as provoking a PRC attack.[114]

Some experts, however, believe that strategic ambiguity has outlived its purpose and should be replaced with "strategic clarity" given cross-strait dynamics.[115] They point to the PRC's continued military build-up aimed at Taiwan and the growing military imbalance in the Taiwan Strait; the political, economic, and military pressure the PRC is exerting on Taiwan; and evidence that Beijing is becoming impatient with the status quo. They argue that strategic ambiguity will not deter an increasingly capable, assertive China that could be tempted to use force against Taiwan. They also believe that placing an equal emphasis on deterring more frequent and realistic island-seizure exercises, and placing greater emphasis on developing information operations (e.g., cyberspace, space-based, and electronic warfare), all of which are geared toward giving it a viable option to use force against Taiwan.[108] These capabilities are intended to challenge the U.S. ability to effectively operate from its fixed bases in the Western Pacific and raise the costs of a U.S. intervention on behalf of Taiwan.

In addition to its growing conventional capabilities, China is rapidly improving and expanding its nuclear arsenal, perhaps convinced that if it can stalemate the United States at the nuclear level, then it can keep a war over Taiwan limited to conventional weapons, where it believes it will soon be able to prevail.[109] DOD assesses that China will

Chinese adventurism and Taiwanese independence (referred to as dual deterrence) is not necessary, as the latter is unlikely to occur, but the former is a more pressing possibility. They assert that a U.S. shift to strategic clarity can and should be made in a way that is consistent with the United States' One China policy. Supporters of strategic ambiguity counter that a change to strategic clarity could provoke the crisis that it seeks to avoid, embolden Taiwan to declare independence, or prompt Taiwan to become a free rider and not take its defense seriously.[116]

The Task Force did not reach a consensus on whether the United States should maintain strategic ambiguity or shift toward strategic clarity. The Task Force did, however, assess that, given the shifting military balance in the Indo-Pacific, U.S. policymakers should no longer assume that PRC leaders believe the United States can or would defend Taiwan. The Task Force concluded that the more pressing issue is for the United States to credibly demonstrate to the PRC that it has the military capacity and the will to come to Taiwan's defense. The Task Force also assessed that, given President Biden's comments on four occasions that the United States would defend Taiwan, his successors should not attempt to walk back these comments and should instead use them as the new baseline for U.S. declaratory policy.

more than triple its nuclear arsenal by the end of this decade, from 400 operational nuclear warheads in 2022 to 1,500 by 2035.[110] According to U.S. Strategic Command, China already has more land-based intercontinental-range missile launchers than the United States.[111] In 2022, Admiral Charles Richard, then commander of U.S. Strategic Command, acknowledged that the PRC could use the nuclear threat during a conflict over Taiwan, stating that they "will likely use nuclear coercion to their advantage in the future."[112]

The war in Ukraine has almost certainly validated China's growing emphasis on having a strong nuclear arsenal: President Biden argued that direct U.S. intervention on Ukraine's side, by pitting two nuclear-armed powers against one another, would result in World War III. Throughout the conflict, the United States and its partners have refrained from providing Ukraine with certain capabilities out of fear that Putin could respond by using nuclear weapons. Xi could hope to deter direct U.S. intervention on Taiwan's behalf through nuclear saber-rattling.

The United States can no longer assume that its direct intervention would be decisive. In addition, as Beijing continues to move the balance of power in the Taiwan Strait in its favor, its cost-benefit calculus is likely shifting. This raises the prospect that at the current trajectory, Beijing will at some point conclude that it could deter Washington from intervening on Taiwan's behalf or hold off the United States should it choose to come to Taiwan's defense.

China does not yet have the ability to invade and seize Taiwan in the face of U.S. intervention, but, barring a significant transformation of Taiwan's military and sustained focus from the U.S. Department of Defense, it will likely gain the capability to do so by the end of the decade.

Despite the stunning advances the PLA has made over the past two decades, it does not yet have the ability to pull off an amphibious assault against Taiwan in the face of U.S. intervention, which would be one of the most difficult military operations in history (see figure 10).[117] Absent U.S. intervention, however, the PLA likely already has the ability to seize Taiwan.

General Mark Milley, chairman of the Joint Chiefs of Staff, has assessed that "it'll be some time before the Chinese have the military capability and they're ready to do it."[118] One recent study organized by the National Defense University and conducted by leading experts

Figure 10

A Chinese Invasion of Taiwan Would Be Operationally Difficult

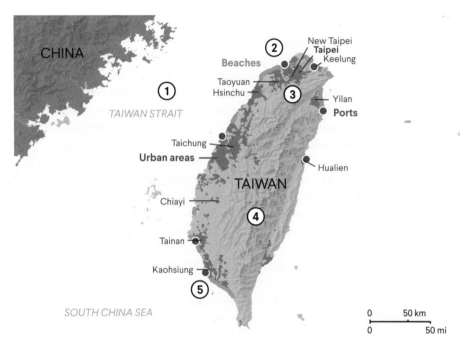

① Rough seas
An amphibious invasion across the 100-mile-wide Taiwan Strait is only feasible a few months out of the year, and PLA vessels would be vulnerable to submarines and anti-ship missiles.

② Few viable landing sites
There are few ports and beaches suitable for a large-scale amphibious assault, due to shallow water, steep coastline with sheer cliffs, and extensive manmade infrastructure near beaches.

③ Population density
Nearly 90 percent of the population lives in 10 cities, which serve as funneling features that aid the defender. China would likely have to conduct urban warfare to conquer the island.

④ Terrain
The island is mountainous, with peaks of over 10,000 feet, which would allow defenders to hide from an invading force and seize the high ground before attacking.

⑤ Strategic chokepoints
Taiwan has few roads, tunnels, and railways that lead from landing sites to major cities, which its military could either defend or destroy.

Sources: Britannica; Bloomberg; Hansen et al., University of Maryland; CFR research.

concluded, "A cross-strait invasion could potentially be decisive but probably lies beyond current PLA capabilities given known gaps in airlift, sealift, and logistics."[119] Other experts emphasize the PLA's lack of combat experience, its unproven ability to conduct combined-arms operations, and deficiencies in its training and logistics support.[120]

Some experts are less sanguine, with one former senior Defense Intelligence Agency official concluding that the PLA has probably already achieved initial capability for a war with the United States over Taiwan.[121] Regardless of disagreements over the PLA's current capabilities, it is clear that China is rapidly addressing its shortcomings and developing a credible military option. Xi Jinping has articulated a goal of building the PLA into a "world-class" military by 2049, which presumably means that he seeks for the PLA to be on par with or even superior to the U.S. military by some measures. Further, the PLA added in 2020 a milestone of accelerating the "integrated development of mechanization, informatization, and intelligentization" by 2027, which marks the one-hundredth anniversary of the PLA's founding.

Many observers have linked this 2027 timeline with a Taiwan scenario. CIA Director Burns noted that the United States knows "as a matter of intelligence" that Xi has ordered the PLA to be ready to invade Taiwan by 2027.[122] DOD has concluded that if China achieves its 2027 aims, it would "give the PLA capabilities to be a more credible military tool for the Chinese Communist Party to wield as it pursues Taiwan unification."[123] Admiral Philip Davidson, when he was commander of U.S. Indo-Pacific Command, was more explicit, asserting, "I think the threat [to Taiwan] is manifest during this decade, in fact, in the next six years" (i.e., 2027).[124] After he stepped down as commander, Davidson publicly commented, "within the next six years they will have the capability and the capacity to forcibly reunify with Taiwan, should they choose force to do it."[125] Taiwan's Minister of Defense Chiu Kuo-cheng, meanwhile, has stated that China will have the ability to conduct a full-scale invasion of Taiwan by 2025.[126]

For years, many observers have pointed to the PLAN's lack of amphibious landing ships and the absence of plans to significantly ramp up the production of these vessels as evidence that the PLA is not serious about invading Taiwan. Such analysis, however, is based on how the U.S. military would conduct such an operation and the capabilities it would need. It does not take into account that the PLA could be taking a different approach, namely, that of utilizing China's massive civilian shipping fleet to transport troops across the Taiwan Strait during a conflict.[127] Indeed, in 2020 and 2021 the PLA practiced using civilian ships during training exercises.[128] As one former senior Defense Intelligence Agency official concluded, there is "nothing in PLA writings on this subject to suggest this is a temporary measure, filling the gap until the Navy expands its own fleet of transports and auxiliary ships. Rather, this seems to be how Chinese leaders, civilian and military, think the PLA should function, leveraging the enormous resources of China's civilian economy to support military operations."[129]

There are additional signs that China is putting into place the pieces it would need to conduct an attack on Taiwan. For instance, in 2022 China introduced a new law that would allow the PLA to more easily call up its reserve forces and replace combat losses during a war.[130] In March 2023, China introduced amendments to the Legislation Law that enable it to pass regulations and laws more rapidly during emergencies; Beijing could use this during a Taiwan scenario to quickly push through a law that provides a legal basis for using force.[131] Although China would need to take several additional steps to prepare for a conflict over Taiwan, such as securing its food supply and stockpiling semiconductors and other critical technologies, these indications suggest that it is becoming increasingly serious about preparing for a conflict.

China is working toward establishing the capacity to invade Taiwan, but it is unknowable whether Xi will call on the PLA to do so. Some observers doubt that there are few, if any, remaining beachheads in Taiwan that could support an amphibious landing, and advocate for exploring this possibility more thoroughly. China's military capabilities, however, are clearer, and the United States and Taiwan need to work under the assumption that Xi could choose to order an attack on Taiwan.

Despite some progress, Taiwan is still not doing enough to address critical shortfalls in its defense and civil resilience.

Historically, Taiwan relied on qualitative superiority to compensate for the PLA's numerical strength. But those days are long gone. The PLA now enjoys qualitative and quantitative superiority over Taiwan's military and the gap between the two sides continues to widen. China has more than 1,900 fighter aircraft to Taiwan's 300, 71 submarines to Taiwan's 2 (although Taiwan has an additional 2 World War II–era submarines, they are only used for training), 45 frigates to Taiwan's 22, and 36 destroyers to Taiwan's 4. In the Taiwan Strait area alone, China has 416,000 ground force personnel, outnumbering Taiwan's ground forces by a ratio of four to one.[132] China's military budget is now over twelve times that of

Taiwan (see figure 11).[133] In addition to its quantitative strength, the PLA now fields nuclear-powered submarines, fifth-generation fighter jets, and other cutting-edge capabilities that Taiwan's military lacks.

Taiwan has failed to keep pace with China, which is understandable given its far smaller population and economy, but what is less forgivable is its failure to use its limited resources more wisely. Too often, Taiwan has prioritized expensive legacy platforms, such as fighter jets, tanks, and large surface vessels, over cheaper, more numerous weapons that can survive and respond to an initial PLA attack. It has purchased U.S. weapons systems designed to project power over great distances and conduct offensive operations rather than investing in cost-imposing defensive schemes. The capabilities Taiwan has prioritized have a role to play in supporting peacetime deterrence by tracking PLA movements in the Taiwan Strait and monitoring PLA activity in Taiwan's ADIZ. Given Taiwan's resource constraints, however, it will need to make difficult trade-offs and has so far largely avoided doing so.

Taiwan's struggles extend beyond military hardware. Its military has a highly centralized command and control structure that does not empower units to make tactical decisions, which means its military would struggle to fight in a degraded communications environment. Taiwan ended conscription but has found the transition to an all-volunteer force difficult and is struggling to meet recruitment targets, especially given its shrinking population.[134] Taiwan's reserve force, as it currently stands, cannot contribute in a meaningful way to its defense, although Taiwan is working to reform its reserves.[135]

Taiwan is belatedly adopting an asymmetric approach to defense that raises the costs of a Chinese use of force.[136] In 2017, its military leadership introduced the Overall Defense Concept (ODC), which calls for shifting emphasis toward a large number of smaller, cheaper, and more mobile and survivable weapons.[137] Rather than seeking to defeat the PLA through attrition, ODC aims to prepare Taiwan's military for a decisive fight near the island's shores and prevent a successful PLA landing. In pursuit of this strategy, Taiwan is developing high-speed attack vessels, ground-based mobile anti-ship missiles, rapid mining capacity, and unmanned aerial systems. It has also purchased the High Mobility Artillery Rocket System (HIMARS) and Harpoon anti-ship, Stinger anti-aircraft, and Javelin anti-tank missiles from the United States.

ODC's implementation, however, has been uneven, and the term was even removed from Taiwan's defense strategy. Some powerful voices in Taiwan, for instance, used the PLA's exercises that followed

Figure 11

The Military Balance in the Taiwan Strait Heavily Favors China

Estimated military assets as of 2022

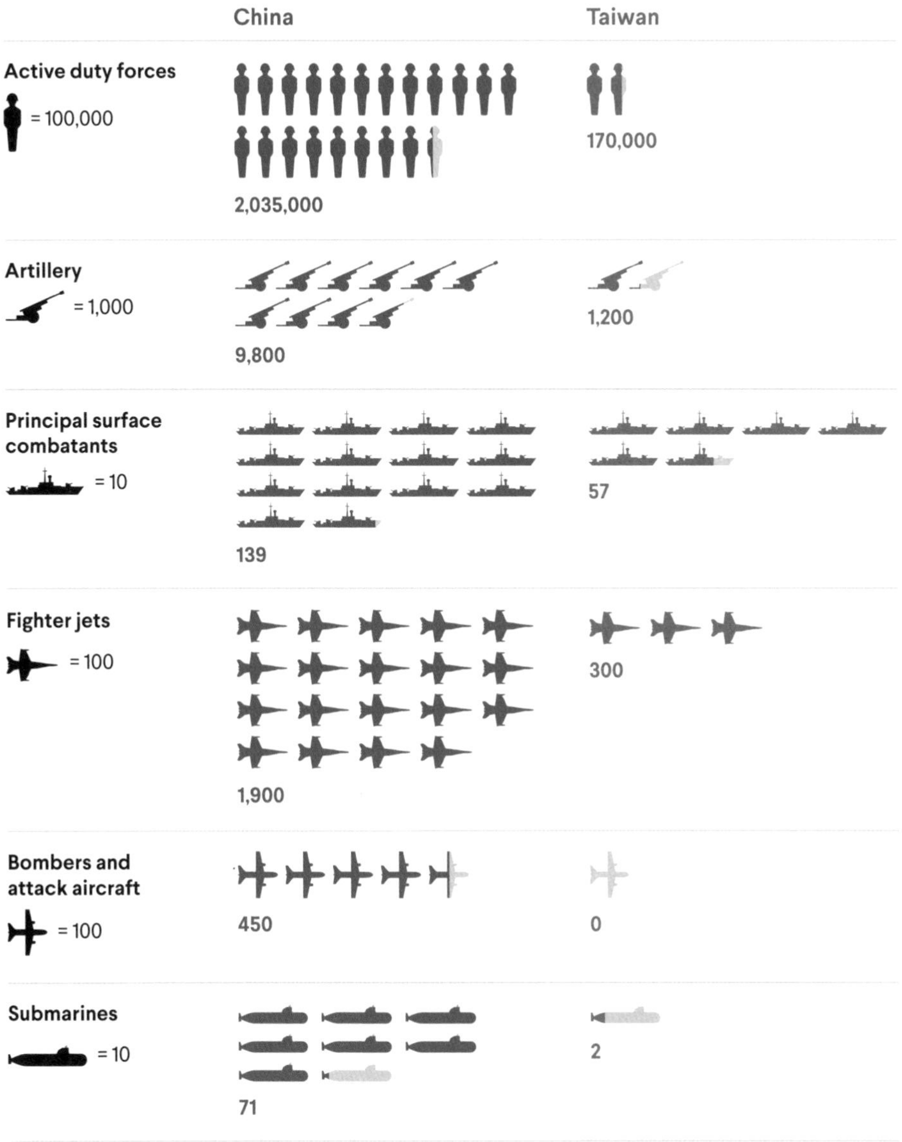

	China	Taiwan
Active duty forces = 100,000	2,035,000	170,000
Artillery = 1,000	9,800	1,200
Principal surface combatants = 10	139	57
Fighter jets = 100	1,900	300
Bombers and attack aircraft = 100	450	0
Submarines = 10	71	2

Source: U.S. Department of Defense.

Speaker Pelosi's trip to Taiwan to argue that Taipei needed to continue emphasizing legacy platforms such as fighter jets and large warships. They asserted that the PLA's activities revealed its preference was to use coercion and potentially a blockade to secure Taiwan's surrender and such weapons were better equipped for dealing with this strategy.[138]

Taiwan has also not prioritized hardening its population's ability to withstand a Chinese blockade or invasion. Taiwan's dependence on imports for 98 percent of its energy supply is a major vulnerability, yet it is shutting down its two remaining nuclear power plants, and its strategy to significantly increase its energy reserves will take nearly a decade to come to fruition.[139] Taiwan's food self-sufficiency has hovered around 33 percent over the past decade, and—despite a goal of boosting this number to 40 percent by 2020—its dependence on imported food remains practically unchanged.[140] A single reservoir supplies the capital of Taipei with 97.5 percent of its water. Taiwan also relies on imported medical and pharmaceutical products, many of which are purchased from China. In 2022, over 70 percent of Taiwan's imports of active pharmaceutical ingredients (APIs) came from China, which represented half of Taiwan's total API supply.[141] Taiwan also depends on China for antibiotics, importing $65 million worth in 2022, accounting for over 68 percent of its total imports.[142] Taiwan also relies heavily on just fourteen undersea internet cables and four cable landing sites to maintain communications with the rest of the world, which China is likely to target early in a conflict and which have already been damaged on multiple occasions by Chinese commercial vessels. China can be expected to exploit these vulnerabilities during a conflict in an attempt to break the will of the Taiwanese people and prevent them from mounting a sustained resistance.

The war in Ukraine, however, has created a sense of urgency for Taiwan's defense reform efforts. Taiwan's 2023 defense budget grew by 14 percent to a record $19.4 billion.[143] Observing the effectiveness of drones and mobile missiles on the battlefield in Ukraine, the Tsai administration is attempting to jump-start domestic drone production and doubling the annual domestic production of missiles.[144] In December 2022, Tsai made the politically difficult decision to extend mandatory military service from four months to one year, envisioning that these personnel would form a standing garrison force whose primary mission would be territorial defense and the protection of infrastructure.[145] Civil society has also taken on greater responsibility; organizations such as Forward Alliance and Kuma Academy are teaching people basic first aid and civil preparedness, with the hope that doing so better enables civilian resistance. Private citizens are also contributing, with semiconductor billionaire Robert Tsao pledging nearly $100 million to improve Taiwan's defense.[146]

Galvanized by Ukraine's example, the Taiwanese people are expressing a heightened willingness to defend their democracy, with a recent survey finding that 70 percent would be willing to fight to prevent a PRC takeover, up from just over 40 percent prior to the war.[147] The more fundamental question, though, is whether they will have the tools to do so. Taiwan's defense spending is equivalent to 2.4 percent of GDP, below what countries facing a similar threat environment, such as Israel and South Korea, spend. Unless significant additional resources are devoted to training those who are serving their mandatory year of military service, these measures are unlikely to meaningfully strengthen Taiwan's combat capabilities and its reserves.

The United States has major military gaps that it is addressing but that would nonetheless make coming to Taiwan's defense difficult and costly.

The U.S. military maintains a significant qualitative edge over the PLA and is committed to maintaining that advantage. With respect to a potential Taiwan contingency, the United States would have notable advantages both in terms of submarine warfare and anti-submarine warfare, the latter of which remains a weakness of the PLA. Although China has developed anti-ship missiles designed to hold U.S. aircraft carriers at risk, there is no guarantee that China will be able to find and hit U.S. carrier strike groups, which offer mobility for U.S. power projection operations. The U.S. Air Force holds an edge over the PLA Air Force, including in stealth capabilities, and could be expected to greatly complicate China's bid to establish air superiority above Taiwan. The U.S. military advantage in theater logistics and battlefield medical evacuation and treatment remains unmatched. Finally, while the PLA has struggled to develop a joint warfare capability, the U.S. military has demonstrated an ability to conduct complex joint operations during wartime.

Geography, however, offers China built-in advantages over the United States in the Indo-Pacific that will be difficult to offset or negate, even with more advanced capabilities. Whereas China is 100 miles away from Taiwan, the closest air base the United States could utilize is in Okinawa, Japan, 460 miles away, while Guam and Hawaii are approximately 1,700 and 5,000 miles away, respectively. The United States has only two air bases from which its fighter jets can conduct unrefueled operations over Taiwan, compared with thirty-nine for China.[148] And the closest U.S. bases are highly vulnerable to Chinese missile attacks. Moreover, if the PLA refrains from attacking Japanese or U.S. territory, there is no guarantee that Japan would allow the United States to operate from bases in Japan during a conflict over Taiwan.[149]

In addition, while the U.S. military has global responsibilities, China's sustained focus on preparing for a Taiwan contingency could mean that it already has an advantage in some respects in the Taiwan Strait. For instance, a 2015 RAND Corporation report that compared the U.S. military and the PLA in the context of a conflict over Taiwan found that the United States moved from having an advantage in most areas to rough parity or disadvantage, with trends continuing to move in China's direction.[150] A more recent study concludes that the United States can prevail against China in a war over Taiwan, but that doing so would come at an enormous cost.[151] Some observers argue that these studies and assumptions need to be taken with a healthy dose of skepticism, given that the PLA has not fought a sustained war since the Korean War and has not seen conflict since 1979. At the same time, however, the United States has spent the past two decades conducting low-intensity counterterrorism operations, not fighting a high-intensity war against a near-peer military.

Due to these challenges, it is incumbent on the United States to have the optimal force posture in the region and ensure that its military services are developing the operational concepts and forces necessary to defeat a Chinese invasion or blockade of Taiwan. The 2022 National Defense Strategy directed DOD to "act urgently to sustain and strengthen U.S. deterrence, with the People's Republic of China (PRC) as the pacing challenge."[152] Assistant Secretary of Defense Ratner went one step further, stating that "a Taiwan contingency is the pacing scenario," indicating that DOD would prioritize the capabilities and force posture it would need to respond to PRC aggression against Taiwan.[153]

The U.S. military services are responding to this top-level guidance by shifting their focus to the PRC. The U.S. Marine Corps, for instance, has introduced Force Design 2030, which aims to develop small, distributed units of Marines that can operate mobile weaponry from remote islands in the Pacific.[154] The U.S. Air Force has invested in stealthier and longer-range bombers, tankers, and long-range munitions, with an eye toward operating at range in the Indo-Pacific. The U.S. Navy is growing its submarine fleet, which could prove decisive during a conflict over Taiwan, and is also developing new unmanned systems. The U.S. Army has developed mobile units designed to quickly deploy and conduct air and missile defense.

Congress is also focused on this issue, and in the fiscal year 2021 (FY 2021) National Defense Authorization Act (NDAA) it created the Pacific Deterrence Initiative (PDI), which aims to improve INDOPA-COM's posture and capabilities to deter Chinese aggression. The following year, Congress authorized $7.1 billion for PDI, and the FY 2023 NDAA authorized an additional $11.5 billion. Importantly, however, PDI is a subset of the Defense Department budget and is not a dedicated appropriations account.[155] In addition, INDOPACOM has put forward a $3.5 billion unfunded priorities list—the largest request of the combatant commands—that includes everything from international security cooperation programs to upgrading missile defenses in Guam and procuring extended-range missiles and other munitions.[156] Thus, more needs to be done to fill important gaps for the U.S. military in the Indo-Pacific.

The United States should continue to arm Ukraine and support its fight against Russian aggression. At the same time, it will need to urgently repair its defense industrial base and prepare for potential contingencies in the Indo-Pacific. The war in Ukraine has demonstrated that modern high-end warfare consumes a tremendous amount of munitions and weaponry, with Ukrainian forces reportedly firing two to four thousand artillery shells per day.[157] The low end of that estimate equates to sixty thousand rounds per month, while the United States is hoping to ramp up its production to forty thousand rounds per month by the spring of 2025.[158] Unless the United States addresses fundamental issues that the war in Ukraine has revealed about the state of its defense industrial base it will struggle to maintain its preparedness for a high-intensity conflict in Asia that would consume enormous amounts of munitions.

Support from allies and partners will be imperative for a U.S. defense of Taiwan, but the level of assistance the United States can expect is largely unknown.

Given the significant geographic limitations it faces, the United States would need support from its allies in the region—above all Japan, but also Australia and the Philippines—if it were to come to Taiwan's defense. Although U.S. allies are beginning to grapple with the implications of Chinese aggression against Taiwan and the need to prepare for such contingencies, the level of support they would ultimately offer is largely unknown.

Japan is both the most essential and potentially willing ally because a Chinese attack on Taiwan poses the starkest threat to its security.[159]

If China were to station military forces on Taiwan, the PLA would be only seventy miles from Yonaguni Island, the westernmost point of the Japanese archipelago, and Japan and the United States would find it much more difficult to defend Japanese territory, including Okinawa. In addition, given that China views the Senkaku/Diaoyu Islands as a part of Taiwan Province, China could attempt to seize them during a conflict over Taiwan. The United States clarified under the Barack Obama, Trump, and Biden administrations that the Senkaku Islands are covered under its treaty with Japan, and thus a Chinese assault on the islands would draw in the United States.

During a full-scale attack on Taiwan, China would also presumably gain control of Pratas Island (which is currently administered by Taiwan), a strategic island adjacent to the entrance to the South China Sea from the Philippine Sea, further cementing the PRC's hold on this critical maritime artery that over 40 percent of Japan's maritime trade passes through. These implications sharpened in August 2022, when China launched missiles in protest of Speaker Pelosi's visit to Taiwan that landed in Japan's exclusive economic zone. For Japan, the day that China absorbs Taiwan would likely be the most destabilizing time for its foreign policy since World War II.

Recognizing these implications, Japanese leaders have been publicly highlighting Tokyo's stake in cross-strait peace. In 2021, Prime Minister Yoshihide Suga and President Biden included a clause on Taiwan in their joint statement, the first time that the two countries mentioned Taiwan in a leader-level joint statement in five decades.[160] Later that year, former Prime Minister Shinzo Abe declared, "A Taiwan emergency is a Japanese emergency, and therefore an emergency for the Japan-U.S. alliance."[161] Prime Minister Fumio Kishida has argued that the "front line of the clash between authoritarianism and democracy is Asia, and particularly Taiwan."[162]

Russia's invasion of Ukraine has further clarified the stakes for Japanese leaders. Kishida drew an explicit parallel between Ukraine and Taiwan, declaring, "We must…never tolerate a unilateral attempt to change the status quo by the use of force in the Indo Pacific, especially in East Asia. Ukraine may be East Asia tomorrow." He added, "Peace and stability in the Taiwan Strait is critical not only for Japan's security but also for the stability of international society."[163] In early 2023, Kishida became the first Japanese prime minister to visit a war zone when he traveled to Kyiv, underscoring Japan's growing willingness to play an active role in geopolitics. In a joint statement with Ukraine's President Volodymyr Zelenskyy, the two leaders "emphasized the importance of peace and stability across the Taiwan Strait as an indispensable element in security and prosperity in the international community."[164]

This major reassessment of Japan's security was formalized in its landmark 2022 national security strategy, which described Japan's security environment as "the most severe and complex…since the end of World War II."[165] Pursuant to that, in late 2022 Japan announced that it would increase its defense budget by 65 percent over the next five years and acquire long-range strike capabilities. In 2023, Japan and the United States made significant strides to evolve their alliance, including the U.S. decision to establish a Marine littoral regiment in Okinawa. In a seeming reference to Taiwan, the countries "renewed their commitment to oppose any unilateral change to the status quo by force regardless of the location in the world." They also "reiterated the importance of maintaining peace and stability across the Taiwan Strait as an indispensable element of security and prosperity in the international community."[166]

In the past year, Japan has moved toward a position of strong opposition to Chinese aggression against Taiwan, but the extent of Japanese involvement in a Taiwan crisis cannot be guaranteed. This uncertainty is largely due to long-standing Japanese constitutional limits on the use of military force for anything other than self-defense. Japan likely also does not want to be more definitive than the United States, which through its policy of strategic ambiguity also declines to state that it would intervene on Taiwan's behalf. At the same time, a more definitive Japanese commitment, even privately conveyed to the United States, would enable greater U.S.-Japan operational coordination.

> For Japan, the day that China absorbs Taiwan would likely be the most destabilizing time for its foreign policy since World War II.

Beyond Japan, it will be important for the United States to enlist Australia's support. Australia has fought alongside the United States in every major war over the past century, and in November 2021, its defense minister stated that it would be "inconceivable" for Australia to not join a U.S. effort to defend Taiwan.[167] In 2022, for the first time, a slim majority of Australians (51 percent) supported using the Australian military if China invaded Taiwan and the United States chose to intervene—an eight-point increase since 2019.[168] In November 2022, President Biden and Australian Prime Minister Anthony Albanese "recognized the imperative of maintaining peace and stability across the Taiwan Strait."[169] The following month, the Joint Statement on Australia-U.S. Ministerial Consultations "reaffirmed their commitment to maintaining peace and stability across the Taiwan Strait and shared opposition to unilateral changes to the status quo."[170]

The United States and Australia have already taken a number of important steps to expand their security ties and deepen their alliance. In 2011, as part of the "pivot" or "rebalance" to Asia, the Obama administration announced that it would rotate U.S. Marines through an Australian base in Darwin, which has expanded from two hundred marines to 2,500.[171] In 2021, Australia, the United Kingdom, and the United States announced a trilateral security agreement (AUKUS), whereby the United States and United Kingdom would support Australia's acquisition of a conventionally armed, nuclear-powered submarine capability. While this ambitious initiative will take well over a decade to come to fruition, if successful, it would bolster deterrence and make a difference during Taiwan contingencies. In the interim, the United States will be increasing its nuclear-powered submarine port visits to Australia and establishing a rotational presence of submarines near Perth. Separately, the United States and Australia have agreed to pre-position munitions and fuel in Australia to support U.S. capabilities. Taken together, these steps will enhance the U.S. ability to respond to PRC actions against Taiwan.

Finally, the Philippines offers critical geographic proximity to Taiwan, as its northernmost inhabited island is only ninety-three miles away, while its waters are optimal for deploying submarines. Until recently, however, it seemed as though this treaty ally would be unwilling to play any role during a crisis in the Taiwan Strait. This posture has changed under President Ferdinand Marcos Jr., who granted the U.S. military access to four additional sites, bringing the total number of sites from which the military can train, pre-position equipment, and build infrastructure in the Philippines to nine. Three of those four new sites are located in northern Luzon, only 160 miles from Taiwan across the Luzon Strait. The Philippines' secretary of foreign affairs, however, clarified that the Philippines would not allow the United States to stockpile weapons at those sites for use in operations to defend Taiwan, nor would it allow the U.S. military to refuel, repair, and reload at those bases.[172]

Nonetheless, Marcos Jr. continues to highlight the connection between peace in the Taiwan Strait and the security of the Philippines. He recently stated, "when we look at the situation in the area, especially the tensions in the Taiwan Strait, we can see that just by our geographical location, should there in fact be conflict in that area…it's very hard to imagine a scenario where the Philippines will not somehow get involved. And not the Philippine military, but we will be brought into the conflict because of…whichever sides are at work. I always remind everyone that Kaohsiung in Taiwan is a forty-minute flight from my province. So we feel that we're very much on the front line."[173] Subsequently, the May 2023 joint statement between President Biden and President Marcos Jr. affirmed "the importance of maintaining peace and stability across the Taiwan Strait as an indispensable element of global security and prosperity."[174] On that same visit, Marcos Jr. did not clarify whether the United States could place weapons at bases in the Philippines during a Taiwan contingency, but did note that they "will also prove to be useful" if China were to attack Taiwan.[175] How far Marcos Jr. will recalibrate the Philippines' foreign policy and how long such a shift lasts, however, remain to be seen.

RECOMMENDATIONS

Politics and Diplomacy

U.S. diplomacy should focus on deterring Chinese aggression, signaling to China and Taiwan that it opposes unilateral changes to the status quo, and ensuring that any future arrangement between China and Taiwan be arrived at peacefully and with the assent of the Taiwanese people. To achieve these goals, the United States should work to increase Taiwan's resilience and ability to counter Chinese coercion. Washington's approach to Beijing should focus both on making clear the risks and costs of using force against Taiwan and on reassuring it that Washington does not seek to permanently separate Taiwan from China. In support of these objectives, the United States should:

Maintain its One China policy while emphasizing that such a policy is predicated on China pursuing a peaceful resolution of cross-strait issues.

The U.S. One China policy is the foundation of modern U.S.-China relations, and its flexibility has also allowed Washington to build a robust unofficial relationship with Taipei. Despite the decades-long success of the One China policy, calls to abandon it and recognize Taiwan as an independent country have recently grown louder.[176] On one level, this position is understandable given that the CCP has never governed Taiwan and the desire to recognize Taiwan's achievements. As the history of negotiations between the United States and the PRC over normalization reveals, however, Beijing will not accept such a course and would sever its relations with Washington if the latter were to recognize Taiwan as an independent country. Animosity

COUNCIL on FOREIGN RELATIONS

58 East 68th Street, New York, New York 10065
tel 212.434.9400 fax 212.434.9800 www.cfr.org

June 20, 2023

Dear Colleague:

As co-chairs of the bipartisan CFR-sponsored Independent Task Force on Taiwan, we are pleased to share with you a copy of the group's consensus report, *U.S.-Taiwan Relations in a New Era: Responding to a More Assertive China.*

As relations between the United States and China enter a new, more perilous era, Taiwan stands as the issue most likely to bring the two nuclear-armed powers and the world's two largest economies into a military confrontation. Although a conflict over Taiwan has thus far been avoided, deterrence has eroded and is at risk of failing. Unless the United States acts to bolster deterrence and raise the costs of aggressive action against Taiwan, the odds of a conflict will increase.

The report proposes that the United States aim to deter Chinese aggression, oppose unilateral changes to the status quo, prioritize Taiwan contingency plans, and support Taiwan's integration into the global economy. The future of one of the world's most critical regions could hinge on whether the United States succeeds in deterring China and maintaining peace in the Taiwan Strait.

We hope you will find it of interest.

Sincerely,

Susan M. Gordon and Michael G. Mullen
Task Force Chairs

between the United States and China would heighten immeasurably, and any attempts to build guardrails between the countries or manage competition would founder. Any prospect of U.S.-China cooperation on global issues from climate change to nonproliferation, however remote, would disappear. U.S. allies and partners, for their part, would view the U.S. abandonment of its One China policy as irresponsible and destabilizing, placing stress on U.S. efforts to enlist their support in balancing China.

A U.S. decision to walk away from its One China policy could also trigger a conflict. China's 2005 Anti-Secession Law threatens, "In the event that the 'Taiwan independence' secessionist forces should act under any name or by any means to cause the fact of Taiwan's secession from China, or that major incidents entailing Taiwan's secession from China should occur, or that possibilities for a peaceful reunification should be completely exhausted, the state shall employ nonpeaceful means and other necessary measures to protect China's sovereignty and territorial integrity."[177] While Beijing purposely leaves these conditions vague, U.S. recognition of Taiwan as an independent country could trigger a PRC use of force against Taiwan.

The current political framework has allowed the United States to pursue its interests with both Taiwan and China, and cross-strait stability it has afforded has enabled Taiwan to prosper and remain secure. Still, while the U.S. One China policy remains the best approach for managing cross-strait relations, the policy leaves enough room for adjustment and should be tweaked. The Taiwan Relations Act states that it is U.S. policy "to make clear that the United States decision to establish diplomatic relations with the People's Republic of China rests upon the expectation that the future of Taiwan will be determined by peaceful means."[178] Senior U.S. officials should publicly and emphatically articulate this linkage between continued U.S. adherence to its One China policy and the PRC refraining from using force against Taiwan—in other words, that the U.S. One China policy is conditional on the PRC's approach to Taiwan. Publicly and consistently making this point would serve as a warning to leaders in Beijing that they should not expect Washington to maintain the status quo if they increase their coercion of Taiwan.

The United States should also seek to establish high-level, regular diplomatic interactions with China with the aim of communicating both the extent and limits of its Taiwan policy and its concerns with the PRC's coercive behavior. In recent years, U.S.-China diplomacy has become too infrequent and too conditional, increasing the risk of misjudgment and miscalculation. Even in an increasingly contentious bilateral relationship, such diplomacy should not be viewed as a favor one side bestows on the other but instead be pursued regardless of the state of relations to further U.S. interests and bring greater transparency to the most sensitive issues, in particular Taiwan. Finally, although decades-long efforts to establish crisis communications mechanisms have faltered, the United States should continue to attempt to establish hotlines to prevent incidents from escalating into full-fledged crises. Whatever their success, good-faith attempts at diplomacy can demonstrate to China, as well as to U.S. allies and partners, that the United States seeks to responsibly manage U.S.-China relations and is not looking to provoke a conflict.

Avoid symbolic political and diplomatic gestures that provoke a Chinese response but do not meaningfully improve Taiwan's defensive capabilities, resilience, or economic competitiveness.

A perennial debate in U.S. policy toward Taiwan is what the balance should be between symbolic versus substantive initiatives. Advocates of pursuing more symbolic steps argue that doing so increases deterrence by highlighting to the PRC the high-level importance the United States attaches to Taiwan. They also emphasize that such steps show the Taiwanese people that they have the support of the United States, thus increasing their confidence. While these are valid points, major symbolic steps are more likely to elicit a strong rebuke from the PRC that targets Taiwan and undermines its security and prosperity. Quiet but substantive steps to build U.S.-Taiwan relations, by contrast, are less likely to provoke a PRC response and can still meaningfully strengthen Taiwan.

The two most symbolic gestures in U.S.-Taiwan relations over the past three decades have also prompted the most forceful PRC responses. When Taiwanese President Lee Teng-hui visited the United States and gave a speech at Cornell University in 1995, the PRC responded by firing missiles near Taiwan's coast, sparking the third Taiwan Strait crisis. In 2022, after Speaker Pelosi visited Taiwan, the PRC conducted its most extensive military exercises to date, fired missiles around and even over Taiwan, and banned hundreds of Taiwanese goods, leading many to term this sequence the fourth Taiwan Strait crisis. The PRC used Speaker Pelosi's visit as a pretext to demonstrate its military capabilities and change the status quo, as it erased the median line in the Taiwan Strait and normalized military activities much closer to Taiwan. In addition, it took the opportunity to spread the narrative that the United States was a destabilizing and provocative actor—an accusation that found purchase in parts of Southeast Asia.

During these same three decades, however, the United States has done much to tangibly build U.S.-Taiwan relations, and those steps that have been kept out of the public eye have not garnered such a strong response. These range from enhanced trade discussions to growing military-to-military cooperation and joint efforts to promote Taiwan's international space. Beijing feels compelled to respond to events that garner international media attention but less urgency to do so when interactions are kept private.

Focusing on substantive improvements in U.S.-Taiwan relations— and not providing the opening that symbolic gestures offer Beijing to alter the status quo—is a more sustainable long-term path for the relationship. It is also worth paying a greater price to pursue needed substantive interactions, for instance enhanced military-to-military ties, but it is often harder to justify the cost of symbolic steps. There could be times when symbolic gestures are warranted; for instance, if the United States believes China is preparing to use force against Taiwan, a high-level visit or visible movement of military assets could be necessary to deter China. The day-to-day management of the relationship, however, should largely be conducted out of the public eye; but such a course will be increasingly difficult, given the deterioration of U.S.-China relations and the desire of politicians to be seen as supporting Taiwan.

Explain to the American people why Taiwan matters and why they should care about its fate.

The United States has a vital strategic interest in defending Taiwan as well as a legal obligation to maintain the capacity to come to its defense and ensure that it has adequate weapons to meet its defensive needs. Many national security professionals appreciate Taiwan's importance to the United States, from its geographic position at the center of the first island chain and its role as the global hub of semiconductor manufacturing, to its willingness to work with the United States as a trusted partner on transnational issues. Those in national security positions also generally appreciate that Taiwan's future will have enormous implications for U.S. alliances in the Indo-Pacific and the United States' position in the world's most economically important region. In a bitterly divided Congress, Taiwan receives overwhelming bipartisan support, making it one of the few unifying issues.

To some extent, the American people grasp the stakes in the Taiwan Strait. According to one recent survey, favorable ratings for Taiwan have never been higher, while a majority of those Americans polled stated that if China were to attack Taiwan they would support imposing sanctions on China, arming Taiwan, and using the U.S. Navy to prevent China from imposing a blockade. The same poll, however, found that only 40 percent of those surveyed would support direct military intervention on Taiwan's behalf.[179] These findings mark a big increase from a decade ago, when only 23 percent expressed support for using military force to defend Taiwan, but still fall short of a majority.

The U.S. government should prioritize educating Americans about why they should care about Taiwan's fate and the effect that a PRC attack would have on their lives and livelihood. Yet no official above the level of assistant secretary of state has devoted a speech to Taiwan since the United States terminated diplomatic relations with the island in 1979. This should change, with a public speech from the secretary of state that outlines the stakes, U.S. interests, and objectives of U.S. policy toward Taiwan. In addition, diplomats in residence should speak about Taiwan at college campuses, and lower-level officials should travel outside of Washington to discuss the issue with Americans.

Create additional international and multilateral forums that allow Taiwan to have its voice heard and contribute to resolving global issues, in a way that does not suggest Taiwanese independence.

Taiwan's international isolation has real costs for the world. In December 2019, Taiwanese health officials heard of people falling sick with a mysterious ailment in the Chinese city of Wuhan and attempted to report it to the World Health Organization (WHO), only to be ignored.[180] Had Taiwan been a full member of the WHO, the organization likely would have been forced to follow up the report, which could have enabled a faster response to the COVID-19 outbreak. Despite being home to one of the world's ten busiest airports, Taiwan is not a member of ICAO, the main international body that oversees international civil aviation. Taiwan is also excluded from the International Criminal Police Organization (Interpol), which facilitates the sharing of data on crimes and criminals, enabling countries to address cross-border crime. China's attempts to exclude Taiwan from international forums also diminishes Taiwanese people's confidence in their government, increasing Taiwan's vulnerability to Chinese coercion. For all these reasons, it is in the U.S. interest to promote Taiwan's meaningful participation in international organizations and even create new platforms to facilitate Taiwan's full membership.

In addition to petitioning UN organizations to include Taiwan in some fashion, the United States has attempted to find creative ways to showcase Taiwan's capabilities and get around its exclusion from international organizations. The most notable example of this effort is the Global Cooperation and Training Framework (GCTF), which was launched in 2015 and convenes workshops to demonstrate Taiwan's expertise in public health, law enforcement, disaster relief, democratic governance, and women's empowerment, among other issues, to countries around the world. Originating as a bilateral U.S.-Taiwan initiative, the GCTF is now jointly administered with Australia and Japan, indicating that additional countries see the benefits of amplifying Taiwan's international voice. In addition, the Trump administration launched the Consultations on Democratic Governance in the Indo-Pacific Region initiative and a Pacific Islands Dialogue platform with Taiwan, both of which aim to assist countries in addressing governance issues and development needs while giving Taiwan a voice.

The United States should pursue a multifaceted strategy to ensure that Taiwan can participate and lend its expertise to regional and global issues. First, it should continue to highlight the costs of excluding Taiwan from organizations such as the WHO, ICAO, and Interpol and press the organizations to include Taiwan as an observer because full membership is not possible. With a realistic understanding that China will continue to block Taiwan's participation in these organizations, the United States should invest more in programs such as the GCTF. It should also reinforce Taiwan's diplomatic partnerships, especially those in the Americas, by pursuing joint development projects with Taiwan. Recalling ambassadors or threatening to withhold aid from countries that switch recognition to the PRC will be less effective than offering to build capacity and contribute to economic development in these countries. Finally, the United States should seek to establish new international organizations that include Taiwan as a full member, such as a new global health entity that is not under the sway of China.

Promote people-to-people ties between the United States and Taiwan.

People-to-people ties, by bringing different populations together through educational and cultural initiatives, help build and reinforce bonds between countries. In the case of U.S.-Taiwan relations, boosting people-to-people ties would help Americans develop a richer understanding of Taiwan's culture and history, while simultaneously providing the benefits of having Americans study Mandarin in Taiwan.

There is vast scope to increase people-to-people ties. Prior to the COVID-19 pandemic, only 23,369 Taiwanese university students studied in the United States per year, while just 1,270 Americans studied in Taiwan. By contrast, during the same academic year, nearly nine times as many Americans studied in China and nearly four times as many studied in South Korea.[181]

The United States has established a range of programs to encourage more exchanges with Taiwan. The U.S. State Department offers the Critical Language Scholarship Program, the Gilman Scholarship Program, and the National Security Language Initiative for Youth, all of which offer Americans the opportunity to immerse themselves in Taiwanese culture and the Mandarin language. The United States sends Fulbright Scholars to Taiwan, a program that continues to grow. In 2020, the United States and Taiwan partnered to establish the U.S.-Taiwan Education Initiative, which expanded existing Mandarin and English language programs in the United States and Taiwan and supported the creation of the Taiwan Center for Mandarin Learning.[182] Taiwan has also opened more than thirty facilities in the United States to teach Americans Mandarin, offering a welcome counterpoint to the PRC's Confucius Institutes, which promote Beijing's political narrative.

Given the urgent need for Americans to learn Mandarin, the State Department's Bureau of Educational and Cultural Affairs and the Department of Education's Office of Elementary and Secondary Education should collaborate with their counterparts in Taiwan's Ministry of Foreign Affairs and Ministry of Education to build a curriculum for middle and high school students. Congress should then offer grants to promote the new curriculum across the country. Indeed, this effort would not only strengthen Americans' interest in Taiwan, but also weaken the influence of PRC education programs like the Confucius Institutes.

Congress should also appropriate funding to the State Department's Bureau of Educational and Cultural Affairs to increase support for cultural and language immersion programs with the express purpose of sending more students to Taiwan. Every year, the Critical Language Scholarship Program, Fulbright Program, Gilman Scholarship Program, and National Security Language Initiative for Youth should send more students to Taiwan. Congress should also appropriate more funding to expand the Taiwan Fellowship Act, which allows ten federal employees to live in Taiwan for a two-year fellowship. This act, established in the FY 2023 NDAA, enables U.S. government employees to study Mandarin and Taiwanese history and politics and then work in a Taiwanese government agency, parliamentary office, or another approved organization. Congress should triple this program to thirty fellows per year.

Economics

The United States has an interest in helping Taiwan reduce its economic ties with the PRC, which is a potential source of leverage that China can exploit during a crisis. In addition, given its heavy reliance on Taiwan for semiconductor manufacturing, the United States needs to ensure that Taiwan remains a trusted economic and trading partner. Yet, despite the compelling rationale to deepen economic ties with Taiwan, already a top ten trading partner for the United States, the economic leg of U.S.-Taiwan relations has been largely neglected. It is past time for an ambitious U.S.-Taiwan economic and trade agenda. In particular, the United States should:

Negotiate a bilateral trade agreement with Taiwan.

In 2021, Taiwan stood as the United States' eighth-largest trading partner, with two-way trade exceeding $114 billion. The United States is also Taiwan's second-largest trading partner, accounting for over 13 percent of Taiwan's total trade.[183] The United States trades more with Taiwan than it does with France, India, Italy, or Vietnam.

Despite this deep trade relationship, a bilateral trade agreement (BTA) has proven elusive, primarily due to U.S. frustration with Taiwan's discriminatory trade policies—specifically, restrictions on U.S. agricultural products. In 2020, however, President Tsai removed the largest impediments, opening Taiwan's market to U.S. pork with ractopamine, as well as U.S. beef products from cattle aged thirty months and older, which had been banned for more than a decade. Despite Tsai's initiative and her strong desire for a BTA with the United States, the United States has not reciprocated. Instead, in June 2022 the Biden administration, after excluding Taiwan from its Indo-Pacific

Economic Framework (IPEF) discussions, announced the creation of a "U.S.-Taiwan Initiative on 21st-Century Trade."[184] Although this is a step in the right direction, the new trade initiative will not cover market access, arguably the most important element of a BTA.

It is past time for the United States and Taiwan to negotiate a comprehensive BTA. Despite opposition to trade agreements in Congress, a BTA with Taiwan has strong bipartisan support and could very well be one of the few trade deals that can be accomplished in the current political environment.[185] Concluding a BTA with Taiwan would have multiple benefits for the United States. The office of the U.S. Trade Representative (USTR) has identified remaining Taiwanese barriers to U.S. agricultural products, as well as restrictions in the pharmaceutical and medical device sectors and issues with copyright enforcement, all of which could be addressed during negotiations.[186] More importantly, USTR can focus trade negotiations on establishing high-standard labor and environmental protections, in the process standardizing and internationalizing those clauses that it incorporated into the United States-Mexico-Canada Agreement (USMCA). A U.S.-Taiwan trade agreement that included such provisions would give the United States greater leverage to include them in future negotiations with other partners.

Although a BTA has economic logic, it has an even more compelling strategic rationale. China is attempting to economically marginalize Taiwan by keeping it out of multilateral trade pacts; Taiwan is not a member of the Regional Comprehensive Economic Partnership (RCEP), and while it has applied to join the Comprehensive and Progressive Agreement for Trans-Pacific Partnership (CPTPP), China has voiced its opposition. China is also pressuring countries not to sign bilateral trade agreements with Taiwan, despite the fact that China signed an Economic Cooperation Framework Agreement with Taiwan in 2010. As a result, Taiwan has only two free trade agreements with countries in the Indo-Pacific, New Zealand and Singapore.

Negotiating a BTA with Taiwan would send a strong signal of U.S. support, boosting Taiwanese confidence in U.S. commitments and in the island's future. It would help Taiwan approach the PRC from a position of strength and also send a message to China that its attempts to coerce Taiwan will not work. Finally, a U.S.-Taiwan BTA would give other countries in the region the cover that they are seeking to negotiate trade agreements of their own with Taiwan, which would in turn assist Taiwan in reducing its economic ties with the PRC. Although countries do not want to be the first to enter such negotiations with Taiwan due to Chinese threats of economic retaliation, more countries would likely be willing to follow on the heels of U.S. initiatives.

Diversify supply chains in critical sectors to reduce the risk from potential Chinese economic retaliation.

A critical difference between the war in Ukraine and a potential conflict over Taiwan is that the United States and its allies are far more reliant on economic ties with China than they were with Russia. They thus risk China concluding that economic sanctions would hurt the countries doing the sanctioning far more than China and that it can act against Taiwan with little risk of being subjected to significant economic penalties.

A few data points illustrate how reliant the United States and its partners are on trade with China. Whereas nearly 7 percent of China's imports come from the United States, 19 percent of U.S. imports are from China. Nearly 8.5 percent of China's imports come from Japan, but nearly 26 percent of Japanese imports are from China. Similarly, nearly 23 percent of the European Union's (EU) imports are from China, but less than 12 percent of China's total imports come from the EU. China is also Taiwan's largest economic partner, accounting for a quarter of Taiwan's total trade and nearly 22 percent of Taiwan's imports.[187] Indeed, most of those countries that the United States would turn to for assistance during a Taiwan conflict—Australia, the EU, Japan, and South Korea—all count China as their largest trading partner.

To this point, much of the focus in Washington and Western capitals has been on reducing their reliance on China for strategic inputs where China holds a dominant market share and reshoring critical industries. For instance, China accounts for 60 percent of global rare earth mining and 85 percent of rare earth processing capacity, giving it control over elements that are crucial for advanced commercial and military products.[188] China refines 68 percent of the world's nickel, 40 percent of all copper, 59 percent of lithium, and 73 percent of cobalt. It is also responsible for most of the world's production of mineral-rich components that are needed for battery cells.[189] And China dominates the market for APIs, which are the primary components of any medical drug.[190]

Focusing on strategic sectors is necessary but not sufficient. Instead, the United States and its allies should conduct a comprehensive assessment of those sectors where China's weight by itself is a cause for concern and coordinate on ways to collectively reduce their economic reliance on China. Although complete decoupling is not feasible or desirable, economically distancing from China is necessary. The United States could help itself by also joining the CPTPP and championing Taiwan's membership in the trade bloc, using this grouping to set high standards for regional trade and promote integration among the United States and its allies and partners. The United States should also assist Taiwan in diversifying its economy away from China by coordinating with Taiwan on its New Southbound Policy that seeks to increase trade and investment ties with Southeast Asia.

Build resiliency in global semiconductor manufacturing.

Semiconductor supply chains have been a model of efficiency, with a typical chip designed in the United States, manufactured in Taiwan, tested and packaged in Southeast Asia, and placed into a product in China or another manufacturing hub before being shipped to customers around the world. This complex global supply chain has allowed countries to specialize in their comparative advantages and ultimately enabled consumers to purchase cheaper products. At the same time, it has created large vulnerabilities. If an earthquake struck TSMC's facilities in Taiwan and forced production of chips to halt, many companies would be unable to source the chips they need. A geopolitical earthquake, which is becoming increasingly likely, would be even more devastating.

The United States needs to walk a fine line, increasing the resiliency of this critical supply chain while enabling Taiwan's world-leading semiconductor manufacturers to continue to thrive. It is unrealistic to believe that U.S. industrial policy can reshore the bulk of semiconductor manufacturing, and pushing too hard for this objective could weaken Taiwan and advantage China. Indeed, the PRC is pushing the narrative through friendly Taiwanese media outlets and disinformation campaigns that the United States seeks to hollow out Taiwan, with the objective of building resentment of the United States and cynicism regarding its intent.

At the same time, the United States should ensure that it has enough manufacturing capacity to produce advanced logic chips at scale for national security, datacenter, and other vital applications. The CHIPS and Science Act is a good start, as was persuading TSMC to establish production facilities in Arizona. To make these bets work, however, the United States will need to bolster efforts to supply the right workers for these facilities. This means reforming its immigration policies to attract and retain engineers, providing more federal funding for basic research and development, and funding educational initiatives that train the types of workers that are needed to operate these plants.

Raise awareness of the economic consequences of a Chinese blockade or attack on Taiwan with allies and partners and coordinate with them to prepare sanctions on China.

China's strategy is to isolate Taiwan and make this a trilateral issue between Washington, Beijing, and Taipei. The economic consequences of a Chinese blockade or attack on Taiwan, however, demonstrate that countries around the world have a stake in cross-strait peace and stability. Simply put, no country would be excluded from the economic carnage of a conflict in the Taiwan Strait, which would throw the world's economy into a severe depression by destroying supply chains, forcing production lines to grind to a halt, sending stock markets plummeting, and threatening global shipping. Once countries are aware of the consequences, and the fact that their economies would not be spared even if they choose to remain neutral during a conflict, they could be more willing to contribute to deterring China from using force.

To raise awareness of the global consequences of a war over Taiwan, the U.S. government should conduct country-by-country analysis of the fallout of a major conflict, which U.S. embassies should then share with host governments. The United States should then work with its allies and partners to prepare a sanctions package that would go into effect immediately following a Chinese blockade or invasion. Policymakers could use the sanctions imposed against Russia following its invasion of Ukraine as a baseline, while also considering more severe financial sanctions. The United States and its allies should preview these sanctions to China, making clear the economic costs of an attack. Although the prospect of sanctions will not be decisive and is likely already factored into Xi's calculus, this strategy would bolster deterrence by demonstrating that sanctions would be deep, immediate, and imposed by many of the world's major economies.

Work with Taiwan to reduce the PRC's economic leverage and respond to its economic coercion.

Taiwan relies far more on trade with China and access to the Chinese market than vice versa, a reality that provides Beijing with leverage over

Taiwan during a crisis. As previously noted, China is Taiwan's largest trading partner, accounting for nearly 23 percent of its foreign trade, a number that increases to 30 percent if Hong Kong is included. Conversely, trade with Taiwan accounts for less than 5 percent of the PRC's total foreign trade. While the PRC needs access to Taiwanese products—above all semiconductors—in order to manufacture many of its exports, if it chose to forcefully pursue unification, it would do so with awareness and acceptance of the economic costs. There is a danger that the PRC concludes that it is better prepared than Taiwan to absorb the economic consequences and can exploit Taiwan's economic reliance on trade with China to force the island into submission.

The United States should urge Taiwan to reduce its exposure to the PRC market and assist it in doing so. Congress should provide the U.S. Development Finance Corporation with additional funding earmarked toward investing alongside Taiwan in Southeast Asia as part of the New Southbound Policy, which aims to rebalance Taiwan's economic ties by increasing its presence in Southeast Asia.

In addition to helping Taiwan rebalance its trade relations, the United States should work with Taiwan to counter PRC economic coercion against the island. To this point, the PRC has banned the import of hundreds of Taiwanese products as well as the export of certain Chinese products to Taiwan. It also pressures Taiwanese businesspeople to publicly denounce and reject Taiwanese independence as a prerequisite to conducting business in China.[191] These steps are all taken to punish Taiwan's government for enacting policies China dislikes and to exact a toll on the voters who supported those politicians.

Thus far, the PRC has refrained from banning those imports that it needs and cannot purchase elsewhere, such as semiconductors and some information and communications technology (ICT) products. For products with available substitutes, however, China has begun to decrease its purchase of Taiwanese products in favor of sourcing from elsewhere. Overall, the economic effects of China's coercion have been relatively limited and largely only felt by the agricultural sector. More significant, though, is that this continued economic pressure threatens to undermine the confidence of the Taiwanese people in their government. It also represents a form of political interference, given that the PRC often targets products and sectors that come from DPP-leaning counties, in an effort to persuade voters not to elect DPP candidates.

Left unchecked, Chinese economic coercion of Taiwan threatens its autonomy and the ability of the Taiwanese people to decide their future.

As substitutes for Taiwanese products become more readily available elsewhere, the PRC will have more leverage to target larger sections of Taiwan's economy and inflict significant economic damage.

The United States should work with its allies and partners to establish an Indo-Pacific Economic Coalition (IPEC), a complement to IPEF that would work to increase economic resilience in the region. In response to any unilateral bans on goods or services, members would consult and decide on multilateral sanctions that they would impose against the aggressor. IPEC does not need dozens of members to be successful: Australia, Japan, the Philippines, South Korea, and Taiwan have all been the target of unilateral Chinese bans, but, along with the United States, they account for nearly 35 percent of the PRC's total imported goods.[192]

Once IPEC is established, the Department of State's Bureau of International Security and Nonproliferation (ISN) should collaborate with the Department of Commerce's Bureau of Industry and Security (BIS) to pinpoint the PRC's most vulnerable industries. Based on the members of the economic collective-resilience bloc, ISN and BIS should determine which sanctions would apply maximum pressure on Beijing. The list of sanctions should then be shared with the United States' IPEC allies to enable a coordinated and collective economic response. Indeed, the economic collective-resilience bloc would act as a deterrent against Beijing's continued economic coercion of Taipei.

IPEC should also have a mechanism to support the victims of China's coercive tactics, which could include a common fund that could make up for lost revenues by purchasing those products as well as a campaign that raises public awareness of China's coercion. For instance, after China banned Taiwanese pineapples in 2021, Taiwan began a campaign advocating for people to purchase its "Freedom Pineapple."[193] The messaging succeeded in garnering the sympathy of many like-minded states: in particular, Japan's consumption of Taiwanese pineapple spiked by 645 percent, more than making up for lost revenue.[194]

Security

Buttressing deterrence in the Taiwan Strait should be the United States' top priority in the Indo-Pacific. If deterrence breaks down and a war erupts, it will be nearly impossible for the United States to pursue its other interests in the region. The war in Ukraine should act as a cautionary tale and inform the U.S. approach to deterrence. Even though the United States has led a coalition to aid Ukraine and punish Russian aggression, the threat of massive sanctions and military assistance ultimately did not deter Putin. In the case of Taiwan, it will be important to lay the groundwork for a sanctions regime ahead of time and preview the costs of aggression to China, but doing so will not be decisive. Instead, only by orienting its military posture in the region for a Taiwan conflict and enlisting the help of its allies can the United States meaningfully alter Xi's cost-benefit analysis and prevent an attack. The U.S. objective should be to ensure that Xi concludes an attack would not succeed and the costs would far outweigh any potential benefits. Achieving this outcome will be difficult but doable with the correct mix of policies. In particular, the United States should:

Prioritize Taiwan contingencies as the DOD pacing scenario and ensure DOD spending supports capabilities and initiatives critical to success, securing the United States' ability to effectively come to Taiwan's defense.

Although the Taiwan Relations Act does not commit the United States to Taiwan's defense, the law does state that it is the policy of the United States "to maintain the capacity...to resist any resort to force or other forms of coercion that would jeopardize the security, or the social or economic system, of the people on Taiwan."[195] Pursuant to this legal obligation, the U.S. Indo-Pacific Command maintains an operations plan to resist Chinese aggression against Taiwan. To continue to meet its legal requirements and ensure that it could defend Taiwan at a reasonable cost, the United States needs to address its gaps with urgency and prioritize preparing for a Taiwan conflict above all other contingencies.

Assistant Secretary of Defense Ely Ratner was correct in identifying a Taiwan contingency as the "pacing scenario" for the Department of Defense. Unfortunately, this specific designation was not included in the 2022 National Defense Strategy. To make this a reality, all of the military services need to develop their capabilities and operational concepts to maximize their effectiveness to deter and, if necessary, prevail in a conflict over Taiwan. DOD should prioritize those capabilities most relevant for a conflict in the Taiwan Strait, principally resilient Command, Control, Communications, Computers, Intelligence, Surveillance, and Reconnaissance (C4ISR), along with space-based assets for a contested environment, long-range anti-ship and anti-submarine missiles, joint air-to-surface standoff missiles, long-range stealth bombers, medium-range ballistic missiles, submarines, electronic warfare capabilities, and networked unmanned systems. It should also focus on distributing its forces throughout the first island chain by increasing its access to Japan's western islands and the Philippines, while hardening U.S. facilities in Guam and Japan.

The most applicable lesson from the war in Ukraine as it relates to Taiwan is that the playbook the United States has used to assist Ukraine would not work in the case of a Chinese invasion of Taiwan. Indirect U.S. support in the form of weapons and intelligence will not be enough; absent direct U.S. military intervention, Taiwan's military likely does not have the ability to resist a Chinese invasion. Thus, preparing for a direct intervention should be DOD's top priority. U.S. officials should also publicly stress that though there are parallels between Ukraine and Taiwan, there are also fundamental differences—above all the U.S. interests at stake in the Taiwan Strait—and thus China should not assume that the United States would limit its assistance to indirect support of Taiwan.

Focusing on a single PRC timeline, whether it be 2027, 2030, or 2049, is a mistake. The fact is that the PLA has been preparing for a Taiwan conflict for decades and will soon have a viable operational plan. One can only speculate about Xi's intentions and sense of urgency, but if he feels compelled to use force because events are moving beyond his control, he could do so even if the PLA is not fully prepared. Therefore, the priority focus should be on strengthening deterrence in the near term, even as the United States continues to invest in building a more robust force structure for the future. The United States needs to be ready to fight now, in five years, and in a decade. Anything less would be catastrophic for U.S. interests and a failure to abide by U.S. law.

Fundamentally shift U.S.-Taiwan security relations to prioritize building Taiwan's self-defense capabilities.

For years, Taiwan's military focused on fighting a conventional war of attrition against China. Thus, it prioritized purchasing F-16 fighter jets to counter China's fourth-generation jets, Abrams tanks to match China's tanks, and large surface warships that could target the PLAN at sea. The United States enabled this approach, selling these legacy platforms to Taiwan, and the U.S.-Taiwan security relationship centered on foreign military sales (FMS). Thus, the United States has sold Taiwan nearly $50 billion of military hardware since 1950, on par with Japan and exceeding Australia and South Korea.[196]

Arming Taiwan, while necessary, is no longer sufficient. Instead, a fundamental shift in U.S.-Taiwan military-to-military relations is required. FMS will still make up a major portion of the relationship, but the United States needs to do much more to build Taiwan's capacity. Currently, Taiwan's military conducts largely scripted exercises, its junior leaders are not empowered to make battlefield decisions, and its training is inadequate. The reality is that only sustained U.S. attention, training, and pressure can change these dynamics. A U.S. program for Taiwan should be no less ambitious than the training that the United States provided to Ukraine from 2014 to 2022, which significantly improved its defensive capabilities and helped enable it to fend off the Russian invasion. Still, it took nearly eight years of sustained investment to build Ukraine's capabilities to this point. A similar process has not yet begun with Taiwan—and it might not have eight years.

Given the sensitivities of sending U.S. military personnel to Taiwan, the United States should focus on training Taiwan's military in the United States, which it already does with Taiwan's F-16 pilots. This has the added benefit of reducing the PRC's ability to collect intelligence on Taiwan's training and capabilities. The United States should invite Taiwan to rotate more and larger units through U.S. facilities for training. The United States should place a particular focus on providing combined arms training to Taiwan's ground forces, which will be critical to defeating a Chinese invasion force. The training should expand to include joint exercises and incorporate Taiwan's active-duty military as well as its reservists. As Taiwan lengthens mandatory military service from four months to one year and overhauls its training methods for conscripts, the United States should offer to help shape this program.

The United States also needs to do more to ensure that it can fight effectively alongside Taiwan's military. Currently, the two armed forces do not have interoperability and would fight separately. To build complementarity, INDOPACOM should establish a common operating picture with Taiwan and standing intelligence sharing platforms, and should invite Taiwan to multilateral exercises such as the Rim of the Pacific (RIMPAC) and Red Flag. Flag officers of up to three-star with relevant portfolios, who would command the numbered fleets and numbered air forces that would lead any fight to defend Taiwan, should visit Taiwan. The United States should also explore expanding the number of American officers who observe Taiwan's military exercises and vice versa.

Given Taiwan's declining population, it could need to rapidly incorporate women into its conscripted force, which it has been hesitant to do. As Taiwan grapples with this challenge, the United States should share best practices with Taiwan's Ministry of National Defense. The U.S. Cyber Command should also establish a high-level dialogue with Taiwan on cyber defenses and offensive cyber capabilities.

Seek greater clarity from allies on the assistance they would provide during Taiwan contingencies and work to improve their capabilities and define roles and responsibilities.

The United States' most notable advantage over China is its strong network of alliances in the Indo-Pacific. The PRC might believe that it could soon neutralize U.S. military power in the Taiwan Strait, but contending with the United States, Australia, and Japan would be an entirely different matter. Although U.S. allies are becoming increasingly open about their willingness to support U.S. intervention on behalf of Taiwan, more clarity is needed so that the United States can begin to discuss roles and responsibilities with its allies and develop a more integrated war plan.

Japan is by far the most critical variable for a defense of Taiwan.[197] Japan hosts fifty-four thousand U.S. troops, who would be called upon to come to Taiwan's defense. These forces would need to be allowed to operate from bases and other installations in Japan. This contingency includes the Seventh Fleet, which is the largest of the

U.S. Navy's forward-deployed fleets and has the United States' only forward-deployed carrier strike group. The United States' only forward-deployed Marine expeditionary force is headquartered in Okinawa (with an air group with operational F-35 and KC-130J squadrons in Iwakuni) and offers a "ready force" capable of responding to a crisis and conducting major combat operations. Kadena Air Base, the United States' largest military installation in the Indo-Pacific not on U.S. territory, is in Japan and is one of only two U.S. air bases (both in Okinawa) from which fighter jets can conduct unrefueled operations over Taiwan. In short, without the use of bases in Japan, U.S. fighter aircraft would be unable to effectively join the fight. The United States would find it nearly impossible to respond promptly and effectively to Chinese aggression against Taiwan without being able to call on these assets and facilities.

Preparing for a conflict in the Taiwan Strait should become a major priority for the U.S.-Japan alliance and should drive force posture and bilateral operational planning and exercises. The United States and Japan should seek to integrate their intelligence, surveillance, and reconnaissance (ISR) capabilities, in particular their space-based assets, and should explore building a common operating picture with Taiwan. In addition, the United States should privately explore with Japan the potential to include Taiwan's military in select exercises. Japan's decision to establish a joint operational headquarters would enable the planning and execution of integrated operations between the United States and Japan. The United States should also seek to leverage Japan's Southwest Islands, rotating troops through those areas and building up ammunition and critical supplies there. The United States should also harden its facilities in Japan and exercise operating from civilian airfields. Most important, the allies should have regular, serious dialogues that allow each side to communicate expectations of the other and pave the way for smooth prior consultation during a crisis.

Beyond Japan, it will be important for the United States to enlist the support of other allies in the region, above all Australia and the Philippines. It is imperative for the United States to ensure that AUKUS is a success, which means expeditiously resolving any export control issues, so that Australia can field a nuclear-powered submarine within a decade and develop a more potent blue water navy. Such a capability would complicate PLA planning, especially given its relative weakness in anti-submarine warfare (ASW). Now with access to nine locations in the Philippines, the United States should build facilities in these areas, pre-positioning ammunition and materiel and rotating troops.

Place the U.S. defense industrial base on a wartime footing now to ensure that the U.S. military has the capabilities it needs to deter Chinese aggression and prioritize arms deliveries to Taiwan.

The U.S. defense industrial base is not prepared for a protracted conflict over Taiwan, a reality that the war in Ukraine has helpfully revealed but also exacerbated. If the United States chose to intervene in a conflict over Taiwan, the U.S. military would require munitions likely in excess of what is currently in DOD's stockpile. In particular, the United States could run out of long-range, precision-guided munitions, which would be crucial to a defense of Taiwan, in less than one week.[198]

The war in Ukraine has highlighted the need for the United States to shift its defense industrial base onto a wartime footing and has begun to galvanize long overdue changes. Still, ensuring that the U.S. military has the capabilities for a war over Taiwan and that it can deliver to Taiwan what it needs will take years, which is why changes need to occur now. The FY 2023 NDAA gave the Defense Department new authorization to award multiyear contracts for certain munitions that are critical for Ukraine and even Taiwan, including PAC-3 air defense missiles, HIMARS, guided multiple launch rocket systems (GMLRS), Stingers, Javelins, long-range anti-ship missiles, and joint air-to-surface standoff missiles.[199] DOD should fully leverage this authority in order to give companies the certainty about a pipeline of orders for which they need to open new production lines. Congress should also expand and fully fund this authority to cover most munitions. In addition, the president should consider invoking the Defense Production Act to create a reserve of essential munitions components.

The assistant secretary of defense for industrial base policy should evaluate supply chains for critical weapons, identifying those that have single points of failure or for which the United States relies on imported components from potential adversaries. There is only one company, for instance, that can manufacture the rocket motor for the Javelin missile, while another single company builds the engines for most cruise missiles. U.S. defense contractors also heavily rely on China for some rare-earth minerals. Congress should appropriate funds to DOD that would enable it to make investments in bringing additional suppliers of critical components online.

Another weakness in the U.S. defense industrial base is shipbuilding, in particular the ability to build and sustain submarines. U.S. submarines would be a critical asymmetric advantage in a conflict over Taiwan, able to target China's amphibious landing force and go largely undetected due to China's shortcomings in ASW. Yet the number of submarines available for such a mission is inadequate.[200] Maintenance delays are a major issue; in FY 2021, the submarine fleet lost nearly 1,500 days while submarines waited for maintenance, an increase from 360 days in FY 2016.[201] This situation will only be compounded by the U.S. Navy's recent decision to temporarily close four nuclear-certified submarine dry docks due to seismic concerns.[202] The United States should seek to incentivize dry dock construction by offering long-term low-interest loans.

The other side of the coin is ensuring that Taiwan has the weapons that it needs pre-positioned on the island before a conflict begins. A critical difference between Ukraine and Taiwan is that it will be much more difficult to resupply Taiwan during a conflict, which means that Taiwan needs to have everything that it needs on the island at the beginning of a conflict. Currently, however, the United States has yet to deliver $19 billion of weapons that it has committed to sell to Taiwan.[203] This backlog includes Stinger anti-aircraft and Javelin anti-tank missiles, as well as HIMARS, all asymmetric capabilities that would complicate PLA planning and execution. The United States has sent so many Stinger and Javelin missiles to Ukraine that it would take thirteen years and five years, respectively, to rebuild the U.S. inventory, which would take priority over delivering items to Taiwan.[204] To mitigate this issue, Congress should appropriate funds to replace equipment that the United States transfers to Taiwan from its stockpiles through Presidential Drawdown Authority, which would enable the United States to more quickly deliver weapons to Taiwan.

Beyond addressing the backlog of arms deliveries to Taiwan, the United States should also pursue coproducing weapons with Taiwan. Taiwan is developing and producing its own unmanned aerial vehicles and ramping up production of its indigenous missiles; the United States should assist Taiwan in optimizing these capabilities.

Conduct a joint study with Taiwan of its war reserve munitions, ability to produce weapons during wartime, and stockpile of essential goods, as well as a separate study on early-warning indicators.

Russia's invasion of Ukraine has demonstrated the munitions-intensive way of modern warfare. Meanwhile, Taiwan's geography underscores the importance of it having significant stockpiles of weapons on the island when a conflict begins. Resupplying Taiwan during a conflict will be extraordinarily difficult; Taiwan will need to be able to fend off a Chinese assault and prevent a fait accompli for long enough to enable U.S. intervention. As of now, however, Taiwan does not have the quantities of vital munitions that it needs.

The war in Ukraine has also reinforced the importance of developing societal resilience. If the PRC blockades Taiwan or strikes critical infrastructure, as Russia is doing in Ukraine, Taiwan will be unlikely to function and remain cohesive for the length of time it would take for the United States to intervene.

The United States and Taiwan should seek to identify critical gaps and create a roadmap to address them. In particular, the two sides should look at Taiwan's existing stockpile of munitions, its capacity to manufacture weapons during wartime (including potential companies that it can repurpose for such an effort), the rate at which Taiwan's military would use munitions during a war, and the percentage that it would lose to Chinese attacks. Beyond weapons, the two should evaluate Taiwan's energy reserves, communications infrastructure, and medical and food supplies. They should discuss how Taiwan can stockpile critical supplies prior to a conflict and how it would ration them during one. The study should also evaluate what the United States would need to supply Taiwan with during a blockade or attack and how best to deliver it. The objective should be to build an understanding of how long Taiwan can likely hold out in the face of a PRC invasion or blockade, to extend that time frame, and to ensure that operations plans are synced with that reality.

Although the PRC is taking steps now to prepare for a conflict in the Taiwan Strait, it would need to make additional, highly visible moves preceding an attack, which would likely include everything from stockpiling and rationing critical goods to moving troops to the coast opposite Taiwan, erecting field hospitals, and requisitioning civilian ships. Ukraine served as an example of how declassifying intelligence and indicators can help raise awareness of an impending conflict and bring together a coalition. The United States should similarly seek to develop a robust set of early warning indicators, in consultation with Taiwan, that it could then publicize prior to a conflict.

CONCLUSION

The United States has vital strategic interests at stake in the Taiwan Strait. Protecting those interests requires that the United States deter a conflict over Taiwan and maintain the capacity to come to Taiwan's defense at a reasonable cost. Given shifts in the military balance of power and China's growing assertiveness throughout the Indo-Pacific, however, deterrence is dangerously eroding, and the United States and China are drifting toward war. At the same time, a conflict over Taiwan is not inevitable. To avoid a conflict that would likely devastate Taiwan, China, and the United States, as well as trigger a deep global depression, the United States should take prudent but firm steps to reestablish a position of strength.

The United States needs to raise the cost of Chinese aggression against Taiwan, with the aim of persuading Xi Jinping that an attack on Taiwan will not succeed and would come at the cost of achieving his modernization objectives. To accomplish this task, DOD should make Taiwan its pacing scenario and resource it accordingly. The United States should make enhancing coordination with Australia, Japan, and the Philippines on Taiwan contingencies a top priority for the alliances, and it should help build Taiwan's military capacity by enhancing training. The United States should also initiate intense consultations with its allies and partners on the scope of a sanctions package that would be introduced immediately after a Chinese blockade or attack, while urgently working to lessen economic dependence on China.

As the United States is taking these steps, it should also make clear that it continues to abide by its One China policy, opposes any unilateral changes to the status quo, does not seek Taiwan's permanent separation, and would support any resolution of cross-strait differences that occurs peacefully and with the consent of the Taiwanese people.

Pursuant to this, the United States should largely eschew symbolic gestures, which are apt to prompt a harsh PRC response and raise concerns in Beijing that Washington is moving away from its One China policy.

Some experts could argue that such steps to bolster deterrence are either too risky or that the costs of a conflict with China are too steep, so the best path forward is to reduce the U.S. commitment to Taiwan and hope for China's forbearance. Such a proposal, however, fails to adequately reckon with what the world would look like the day after the PRC forcefully annexed Taiwan. Above all, it would be a tragedy for Taiwan's twenty-three million citizens and one of Asia's freest societies. For the United States, it would also mean the loss of an important partner and vastly diminished influence in the world's most economically important region. China would be able to project power far beyond its shores, limiting the United States' ability to operate in the Indo-Pacific and posing a greater threat to U.S. allies, who would come to question their reliance on the United States. The United States cannot wish away the stakes and instead needs a bolder strategy to protect its vital strategic interests in the Taiwan Strait.

ADDITIONAL AND DISSENTING VIEWS

Although I concur with most of the report and its recommendations, I think its emphasis on military deterrence comes at the expense of sufficient attention to the nonmilitary aspects of both the problem and its potential mitigation. The Taiwan issue is not primarily a military problem; it is fundamentally a political dilemma that will require concerted diplomatic efforts to avoid military conflict. And although the report acknowledges that military deterrence should be supplemented by reassurances to Beijing "that Washington does not seek to permanently separate Taiwan from China," it does not sufficiently address the challenge that Washington faces in making such assurances credible.

In this regard, the report recommends that Washington "maintain its One China policy," but without meaningfully confronting widespread concerns about the erosion of the substance and credibility of that policy. That erosion, however, is one of the main drivers of crossstrait tensions. The report explains how "the U.S. One China policy has evolved over time," with incremental upgrades in U.S.-Taiwan relations that have stretched the limits of "unofficial" ties. Moreover, Taiwan's own position on "one China" has evolved over time, and Beijing views Washington's tacit acceptance of this change as implicit endorsement of Taipei's apparent efforts to retreat from the "one China" framework. In short, there are valid questions about whether Washington is moving toward a de facto "one China, one Taiwan" policy in violation of U.S. commitments under the Three Communiqués. This is why U.S. reassurances to the contrary need to be more substantive and credible than the rhetorical reaffirmation that the One China policy has not changed.

The report attributes cross-strait tensions almost exclusively to "a more powerful and assertive China" and uncertainty about Xi Jinping's intentions. But this assessment overlooks the extent to which Beijing's behavior has been reactive to steps by Washington and Taipei that have themselves altered "the status quo" and weakened the "one China" framework. In this regard, I disagree with the report's recommendation that Washington should use President Biden's public comments about defending Taiwan "as the new baseline for U.S. declaratory policy."

Finally, the report invokes Assistant Secretary of Defense Ely Ratner's statement during congressional testimony in December 2021 that Taiwan is a "critical node" in the "defense of vital U.S. interests in the Indo-Pacific." But this historically new formulation would appear to provide a geostrategic military rationale for supporting Taiwan's permanent separation from China—contrary to the reassurances that the report advises Washington to make to Beijing. This further underscores the importance of making those assurances substantive and credible.

In sum, the report appropriately advises Washington to make clear to Beijing that "the U.S. One China policy is conditional on the PRC's approach to Taiwan." But Washington should also recognize the obverse: that Beijing's cross-strait behavior will be conditional on Washington's own evolving approach to Taipei.

—*Paul Heer*

A Leninist political organization, the CCP needs hostile foreign forces—real or imagined—to justify the continued dictatorship of the party. Beijing cooperated with Washington in the 1980s to isolate the Soviet Union. But with the USSR's demise in 1991, the CCP returned to casting the United States as its principal existential threat—at first internally, and now openly. The Task Force found that China is convinced the United States "is actively endorsing or implicitly emboldening an independence movement in Taiwan, and that U.S. support for Taiwan remains the primary obstacle standing between China and its ability to achieve unification."

It would be wrong to conclude that a policy of reassurance by Washington, rather than deterrence, would reduce Beijing's appetite for changing the status quo through force.

For many years, Washington tried to reassure both Putin and Xi by eschewing "provocative" actions; both dictators seized the opportunity to expand territorial control at the expense of other nations' sovereignty and to the detriment of international conventions and norms. Moscow saw Washington suspend the provision of defensive weapons to Ukraine in 2021 and was emboldened. In the 2010s, Beijing saw Washington provide only tepid support for allies' assertion of their maritime rights, and the PLA seized a South China Sea feature and built an expeditionary base within the Philippines' exclusive economic zone. Starting in 2010, Washington suspended new sales of platforms and munitions to Taiwan for seventy months, and Beijing has answered by moving aggressively to upend a peaceful status quo in the Taiwan Strait.

As the Leninist adage goes, "You probe with bayonets: if you find mush, you push. If you find steel, you withdraw."

U.S. actions more recently are becoming a bit less mushy and a bit steelier. American credibility increased with President Biden's spoken commitment to defend Taiwan against aggression and Speaker Pelosi's resolve to visit Taipei despite an extensive CCP influence campaign against her. Had Washington buckled, questions about U.S. reliability would again have taken center stage. Allies and partners will similarly lose faith—and Beijing will be emboldened—if a U.S. president walks back the defense commitment in the future.

In addition to military power, Taiwan's political, economic, and societal connections to other countries also enhance deterrence by increasing the costs and multiplying the victims of potential aggression. Senior officials from several allied countries have streamed into Taiwan following Pelosi. In April, when China announced missile tests in air corridors near Taiwan for eighteen hours over three days—which would have diverted hundreds of commercial flights—Taiwan, Japan, and other nations told China they would not accept such a move. Beijing backed down, reducing the disruption to a single twenty-seven-minute block.

Xi knows he is the one upending the status quo—he said as much to Putin in March. Beijing cannot be reassured because it is not really seeking reassurance. It is probing with bayonets for weakness, hoping for accommodation and concession. Maintaining the United States' status as a global power depends on Washington showing steely resolve to deny Beijing the chance to coerce Taiwan into submission.

—*Ivan Kanapathy and Matthew Pottinger*

While I support many of the findings and recommendations of this report, it falls short on the following three issues.

First, at a time when threat perceptions of China are (understandably) high in the United States and the political incentives are strong for leaders to out-hawk each other on China, the report could more forcefully dispel the simplistic view that any moderation of U.S. words and actions around Taiwan is tantamount to "appeasement" that invites Chinese aggression. The report wisely points out that Washington should avoid symbolic gestures that "provoke a Chinese response" but do not "meaningfully strengthen" Taiwan's resilience. It cites Speaker Pelosi's visit to Taiwan as one such example that gave Beijing the opportunity to frame Washington as a destabilizing actor, and that this characterization "found purchase in parts of Southeast Asia." But the reality is that this view was widespread, if not publicly admitted, among many U.S. allies and partners, including in *Taiwan*, where polling found that a majority viewed the visit as detrimental to Taiwan's security.[205] U.S. allies and partners, including the Taiwanese people, expect the United States to judiciously handle the sensitivities and stakes involved for all parties in the Taiwan Strait. This is not a sign of "weakness" but of smart diplomacy that takes Taiwan's overall welfare into account, keeps allies and partners on our side, and reduces unnecessary friction with Beijing.

Second, the report states as fact that as Xi "approaches the end of his tenure," the basis of his legitimacy will "shift from delivering economic growth to satisfying Chinese nationalism," and thus increase the probability of a Chinese invasion of Taiwan. It is unclear what the factual basis is for forecasting such a chain of events. The report takes this leap after citing China's *relative* economic slowdown and Xi's statements about "unification" with Taiwan as being essential for China's "rejuvenation." But it neglects to consider the immense consequences China would face upon launching an assault on Taiwan—from the likely loss of thousands of troops and significant decimation of military assets to economic and diplomatic isolation from, at the very least, the advanced economies of the world, all of which would fundamentally undermine China's "rejuvenation" project and national pride that are deeply intertwined with its continued economic prosperity and stability. Failing to recognize the mutual vulnerability of all parties, including China's, misleadingly suggests that Beijing is invulnerable and undeterrable, and only serves as a propaganda win for Xi.

Finally, while the risks of a clash with China in the Taiwan Strait are indeed growing, a Taiwan contingency should be prioritized as *a* pacing scenario for DOD, rather than *the* pacing scenario as the report recommends. This distinction is critical given growing voices from some political quarters that assert Washington should not be "distracted" by Moscow or engaged in other regions. But U.S.-China competition cannot be neatly contained to the Taiwan Strait, and Beijing is far from the only destabilizing actor in the international arena. Bestowing such a designation would send the wrong signal to adversaries and allies alike.

—*Patricia M. Kim*

I endorse the report because I support "the general policy thrust and judgments reached by the group." While endorsement comes with the caveat that it does "not necessarily" mean support for "every finding and recommendation," I write separately first to express discomfort with the report's dominant military thrust and assessment of a new baseline for strategic ambiguity. Second, although the report lists "democracy" among important U.S. interests, democracy is an inadequate shorthand for "human rights."

The deep military expertise of Task Force members underscored the need for robust deterrence in preserving peace and stability in the Taiwan Strait. Alongside this military framing, the report recommends that Washington "maintain its One China policy" and states that "Washington's approach to Beijing should focus both on making clear the risks and costs of using force against Taiwan *and* reassuring it that Washington does not seek to permanently separate Taiwan from China" (emphasis added). To be sure, the United States' One China policy is not inflexible, but the recommendation that it "should be tweaked" to make clear that it "is conditional on the PRC's approach to Taiwan" is not accompanied by adequate grappling with how tweaking can erode Beijing's confidence in Washington's intentions.

The Task Force did not reach a consensus on strategic ambiguity. The report stresses that the "pressing issue is for the United States to credibly demonstrate to the PRC that it has the military capacity and the will to come to Taiwan's defense. The Task Force also assessed that, given President Biden's comments on four occasions that the United States would defend Taiwan, his successors should not attempt to walk back these comments and should instead use them as the new baseline for U.S. declaratory policy". I agree with the first sentence, but the second goes too far in setting a new baseline that explicitly incorporates Biden's comments, especially given his suggestion that the United

States is bound to defend Taiwan in the same manner as defense treaty commitments to Japan and South Korea.

The report lists "democracy" among important U.S. interests. I would go further to emphasize that not only is democracy a universal value of the United Nations, but there is also a broad range of human rights, from equality to freedom of expression, that deserve highlighting. The phrase "human rights" is implicit in the report but should be explicit. The people of Taiwan fought long and hard to enjoy a panoply of rights, and China's coercion threatens both the rights of people in Taiwan and the strength of universal norms.

Finally, I wholeheartedly endorse the calls for bolstering communication through "high-level, regular diplomatic interactions with China" as well as promoting "people-to-people ties between the United States and Taiwan." Yet even more is needed: namely, enhanced communication channels among the United States, China, and Taiwan from high-level official interactions to low-level unofficial ones. Continuous, multivarious information flows into the policymaking process are essential to preserving peace and stability in the Taiwan Strait.

—Margaret K. Lewis

Firstly, this report, for all its merits, understates the point that deterrence is composed not only of measures that convince the PRC that military action to subjugate Taiwan would come at too high a cost and with a significant risk of failure, but also of measures that convince the PRC that such action is not needed for the time being. Actions and signals by Washington that Beijing interprets as confirmation that the United States remains prepared to accept unification, so long as it is peaceful and on terms agreed upon by China and Taiwan—a position at the heart of the U.S. One China policy—helps to mitigate fear that the "window" for unification is closing and therefore to diminish the sense of urgency that fosters risk-taking. At the same time, signals that Taipei is not ruling out a future dialogue with Beijing where options for political compromise could be explored would also contribute to deterrence.

Secondly, it is important to recognize that an insistence by U.S. officials that Taiwan must be "retained" as a strategic military asset and denied to the PRC contradicts the principle embedded in the One China policy that the future arrangement is for the people on both sides of the Taiwan Strait to decide. The United States might take the position that ultimately no PLA forces should be deployed to Taiwan after a settlement, but that is a different argument.

Lastly, the report rightly points to the risk of gray zone aggression short of war, particularly the imposition of a quarantine or blockade based on sophistry and "lawfare" claiming PRC rights to the air and sea around Taiwan. But a much more urgent call to action is needed if Taiwan and its partners are to develop timely countermeasures that can check PRC moves in this direction and ensure resilience through adequate stockpiles of essential civil resources.

—Daniel R. Russel
joined by Douglas H. Paal

ENDNOTES

1. Ben Blanchard, "U.S. Should Recognize Taiwan, Former Top Diplomat Pompeo Says," Reuters, March 4, 2022, https://www.reuters.com/world/asia-pacific/us-should-recognise-taiwan-former-top-diplomat-pompeo-says-2022-03-04; Lawrence Chung, "Former US Defense Chief Says One-China Policy Has 'Outlived Its Usefulness,'" *South China Morning Post*, July 19, 2022, https://www.scmp.com/news/china/diplomacy/article/3185818/former-us-defence-chief-says-one-china-policy-has-outlived-its.

2. Mark F. Cancian, Matthew Cancian, and Eric Heginbotham, *The First Battle of the Next War: Wargaming a Chinese Invasion of Taiwan* (Washington, DC: Center for Strategic and International Studies, 2023), https://www.csis.org/analysis/first-battle-next-war-wargaming-chinese-invasion-taiwan.

3. Franklin D. Roosevelt, Winston Churchill, and Chiang Kai-shek, "The Cairo Declaration," press communiqué, November 26, 1943, https://digitalarchive.wilsoncenter.org/document/cairo-declaration. In this declaration, Roosevelt, Churchill, and Chiang stated "that Japan, shall be stripped of all the islands in the Pacific which she has seized or occupied since the beginning of the first World War in 1914, and that all the territories Japan has stolen from the Chinese, such as Manchuria, Formosa, and the Pescadores, shall be restored to the Republic of China."

4. Harry S. Truman, Winston Churchill, and Chiang Kai-shek, "Proclamation by the Heads of Governments, United States, China, and the United Kingdom," proclamation no. 1382 (July 26, 1945), *Foreign Relations of the United States: Diplomatic Papers, Proclamation 1382 of 1945, Conference of Berlin (The Potsdam Conference) 1945,* vol. 2, ed. Richardson Dougall (Washington, DC: Government Printing Office, 1960), https://history.state.gov/historicaldocuments/frus1945Berlinv02/d1382. The Potsdam Declaration specified, "The terms of the Cairo Declaration shall be carried out and Japanese sovereignty shall be limited to the islands of Honshu, Hokkaido, Kyushu, Shikoku and such minor islands as we determine."

5. This discussion of U.S.-Taiwan relations draws on Alan D. Romberg, *Rein In at the Brink of the Precipice: American Policy Toward Taiwan and U.S.-PRC Relations* (Washington, DC: Stimson Center, 2003).

6. The best book on this chapter of history is Daniel Kurtz-Phelan, *The China Mission: George Marshall's Unfinished War, 1945–1947* (New York: W.W. Norton, 2018).

7. Qin Gang, Ministry of Foreign Affairs of the People's Republic of China, "Foreign Minister Qin Gang Meets the Press," (press conference, Beijing, March 7, 2023), https://www.fmprc.gov.cn/mfa_eng/wjb_663304/wjbz_663308/2461_663310/202303/t20230307_11037190.html.

8. State Council Taiwan Affairs Office and Information Office, "The One-China Principle and the Taiwan Issue," white paper, February 21, 2000, http://www.taiwandocuments.org/white.htm.

9. On January 5, 1950, President Truman issued that the following statement: "The United States Government will not pursue a course which will lead to involvement in the civil conflict in China. Similarly, the United States Government will not provide military aid or advice to Chinese forces on Formosa." Romberg, *Rein In at the Brink*, 2.

10. Romberg, *Rein In at the Brink*, 2.

11. U.S. Department of State, "Memorandum of Conversation," Beijing, July 9, 1971, in *Foreign Relations of the United States, 1969–1976*, vol. 17, China, 1969–1972, ed. Stephen E. Phillips (Washington, DC: Government Printing Office, 2006), https://history.state.gov/historicaldocuments/frus1969-76v17/d139.

12. Harry S. Truman, "Statement Issued by the President," document 119, June 27, 1950, in *Foreign Relations of the United States, 1950,* vol. 7, ed. John P. Glennon (Washington, DC: Government Printing Office, 1976), 202–203.

13. Romberg, *Rein In at the Brink*, 29–41.

14. American Institute in Taiwan, "U.S.-PRC Joint Communiqué (1979)," January 1, 1979, https://www.ait.org.tw/u-s-prc-joint-communique-1979.

15. Taiwan Relations Act, H.R. 2479, 96th Cong. (1979), https://www.ait.org.tw/policy-history/taiwan-relations-act.

16. American Institute in Taiwan, "U.S.-PRC Joint Communiqué (1982)," August 17, 1982, https://www.ait.org.tw/u-s-prc-joint-communique-1982.

17. Romberg, *Rein In at the Brink*, 132.

18. George Shultz, "Declassified Cables: Taiwan Arm Sales and Six Assurances (1982), Assurance for Taiwan Cable," declassified cable, August 17, 1982, https://www.ait.org.tw/declassified-cables-taiwan-arms-sales-six-assurances-1982.

19. George Shultz, "Declassified Cables."

20. For more on the U.S. One China policy, see Richard C. Bush, *A One-China Policy Primer* (Washington, DC: Brookings Institution, 2017), https://www.brookings.edu/research/a-one-china-policy-primer; Alan D. Romberg, "The U.S. 'One China' Policy: Time for a Change?," Charles Neuhauser Memorial Lecture at the John K. Fairbank Center of Harvard University, October 24, 2007, https://www.stimson.org/2007/us-one-china-policy-time-change; and Shirley Kan, "China/Taiwan: Evolution of the 'One China' Policy—Key Statements From Washington, Beijing, and Taipei," *Congressional Research Service*, October 10, 2014, https://sgp.fas.org/crs/row/RL30341.pdf.

21. Multiple senior officials have made this point over the years. For instance, Secretary of State Warren Christopher asserted, "our 'one China' policy is predicated on the PRC's pursuit of a peaceful resolution of the issues between Taipei and Beijing." Romberg, *Rein In at the Brink*, 177.

22. Kan, "China/Taiwan," 69.

23. Office of the Press Secretary (Shanghai, People's Republic of China), "Remarks by the President and the First Lady in Discussion on Shaping China for the 21st Century," Shanghai Library, June 30, 1998, https://clintonwhitehouse6.archives.gov/1998/06/1998-06-30-remarks-by-president-and-first-lady-at-shanghai-library.html.

24. The Foreign Relations Authorization Act for Fiscal Year 2003, H.R. 1646, September 30, 2002, sec. 326, https://www.congress.gov/107/plaws/publ228/PLAW-107publ228.pdf.

25. For instance, President Nixon privately reassured Premier Zhou Enlai, "There is one China, and Taiwan is a part of China. There will be no more statements made—if I can control our bureaucracy—to the effect that the status of Taiwan is undetermined." White House, Memorandum of Conversation, The National Security Archive, George Washington University, February, 22 1972, https://nsarchive2.gwu.edu/NSAEBB/NSAEBB106/NZ-1.pdf; see also Romberg, *Rein In at the Brink*, 19–48; for the full text of the Shanghai Communiqué, see American Institute in Taiwan, "U.S.-PRC Joint Communiqué (1972)," February 28, 1972, https://www.ait.org.tw/u-s-prc-joint-communique-1972; for the full text of the Normalization Communiqué, see American Institute in Taiwan, "U.S.-PRC Joint Communiqué 1979)," January 1, 1979, https://www.ait.org.tw/u-s-prc-joint-communique-1979.

26. U.S. Department of State, "Memorandum of Conversation," Beijing, October 21, 1975, in *Foreign Relations of the United States, 1969–1976*, vol. 18, China, 1973–1976, ed. David P. Nickles (Washington, DC: Government Printing Office, 2007), https://history.state.gov/historicaldocuments/frus1969-76v18/d124. For instance, Mao Zedong privately stated that China could wait one hundred years to settle the question of Taiwan's status. Deng Xiaoping echoed this statement on June 22, 1984, remarking, "Achieving national unification is the nation's wish, if not unified in 100 years, then unified in 1,000 years." For Deng's remarks in full, see Deng Xiaoping, "One Country, Two Systems," *Selected Works of Deng Xiaoping*, vol. 3 (1982–1992) (Beijing: Foreign Languages Press, 1994).

27. Richard C. Bush, *At Cross Purposes: U.S.-Taiwan Relations Since 1942* (New York: Routledge, 2015), 85–123.

28. Shelley Rigger, *The Tiger Leading the Dragon: How Taiwan Propelled China's Economic Rise* (Lanham, MD: Rowman and Littlefield, 2021).

29. Government Portal of the Republic of China (Taiwan), "Cross-Strait Relations: Fact Focus," accessed on April 29, 2023, https://www.taiwan.gov.tw/content_6.php#.

30. Bureau of Foreign Trade, "Trade Statistics: Introduction—Exports," Ministry of Economic Affairs, Republic of China (Taiwan), accessed April 22, 2023, https://cuswebo.trade.gov.tw/FSCE000F/FSCE000F.

31. International Monetary Fund, World Economic Outlook Database (for October 2022), accessed April 23, 2023, https://www.imf.org/en/Publications/WEO/weo-database/2022/October.

32. State Council, "China Releases White Paper on Taiwan Question, Reunification in New Era," news release, People's Republic of China, August 2022, https://english.www.gov.cn/archive/whitepaper/202208/10/content_WS62f34f46c6d02e533532f0ac.html (hereinafter PRC State Council, "Taiwan Question"). A link to download the full text of the white paper, titled "The Taiwan Question and China's Reunification in the New Era," is at the end of this news release.

33. National Chengchi University Election Study Center, "Taiwan Independence vs. Unification With the Mainland (1994/12–2022/06)," January 13, 2023, https://esc.nccu.edu.tw/PageDoc/Detail?fid=7801&id=6963.

34. Timothy Rich and Andi Dahmer, "Taiwan Opinion Polling on Unification With China," *China Brief* 20, no. 18 (October 2020), https://jamestown.org/program/taiwan-opinion-polling-on-unification-with-china.

35. Shelley Rigger, Lev Nachman, Chit Wai John Mok, and Nathan Kar Ming Chan, "Why Is Unification So Unpopular in Taiwan? It's the PRC Political System, Not Just Culture," Brookings Institution, February 7, 2022, https://www.brookings.edu/blog/order-from-chaos/2022/02/07/why-is-unification-so-unpopular-in-taiwan-its-the-prc-political-system-not-just-culture.

36. Michael R. Pompeo, "Lifting Self-Imposed Restrictions on the U.S.-Taiwan Relationship," press statement, U.S. Department of State, January 9, 2021, https://2017-2021.state.gov/lifting-self-imposed-restrictions-on-the-u-s-taiwan-relationship/index.html.

37. Blanchard, "U.S. Should Recognize Taiwan"; Chung, "Former US Defense Chief Says."

38. The bill expressed "the sense of Congress that the United States should resume normal diplomatic relations with Taiwan, negotiate a bilateral free trade agreement with Taiwan, and support Taiwan's membership in international organizations." H. Con. Res. 21, 117th Cong. (2021).

39. Ministry of Foreign Affairs of the People's Republic of China, "Wang Yi Meets With U.S. Secretary of State Antony Blinken," news release, October 31, 2021, https://www.fmprc.gov.cn/mfa_eng/wjb_663304/wjbz_663308/activities_663312/202111/t20211101_10435630.html; Ministry of Foreign Affairs of the People's Republic of China, "Wang Yi: The U.S. Side's Act in Bad Faith on the Taiwan Question Will Only Further Bankrupt Its National Credibility," news release, August 3, 2022, https://www.fmprc.gov.cn/mfa_eng/zxxx_662805/202208/t20220803_10732397.html.

40. CCCTV, "Spokesperson Slams Taiwan DPP's 'de-Sinicization' History-Distorting Textbook," October 14, 2021, https://english.cctv.com/2021/10/14/ARTIhnkXtmEUFexaeygVPEfw211014.shtml; Katherine Wei, "Taiwan 'Playing Little Tricks' With New Passport Design, Says China," *Straits Times*, January 12, 2021, https://www.straitstimes.com/asia/east-asia/taiwan-introduces-new-passport-design-to-differentiate-it-from-chinas.

41. Ministry of Foreign Affairs, "Wang Yi Meets With U.S. Secretary of State."

42. National Chengchi University Election Study Center, "Taiwanese/Chinese Identity (1992/06-2022/12)," accessed April 22, 2023, https://esc.nccu.edu.tw/PageDoc/Detail?fid=7800&id=6961.

43. Louisa Brooke-Holland, "Hong Kong: The Joint Declaration," briefing paper no. 08616, House of Commons Library, United Kingdom, July 5, 2019, https://researchbriefings.files.parliament.uk/documents/CBP-8616/CBP-8616.pdf.

44. PRC State Council, "Taiwan Question."

45. Richard C. Bush, "8 Key Things to Notice From Xi Jinping's New Year Speech on Taiwan," Brookings Institution, January 7, 2019, https://www.brookings.edu/blog/order-from-chaos/2019/01/07/8-key-things-to-notice-from-xi-jinpings-new-year-speech-on-taiwan.

46. Ben Blanchard, Michael Holden, and Venus Wu, "China Says Sino-British Joint Declaration on Hong Kong No Longer Has Meaning," Reuters, June 30, 2017, https://www.reuters.com/article/us-hongkong-anniversary-china/china-says-sino-british-joint-declaration-on-hong-kong-no-longer-has-meaning-idUSKBN19L1J1.

47. Robbie Gramer, "Chinese Delegation Blows Up at Anti-Conflict Diamond Meeting to Sideline Taiwan," *Foreign Policy*, May 2, 2017, https://foreignpolicy.com/2017/05/02/china-delegation-taiwan-australia-conflict-minerals-meeting-one-china-policy-diplomatic-dispute-kimberley-process.

48. Javier C. Hernández, "Latest Clash Between China and Taiwan: A Fistfight in Fiji," *New York Times*, October 19, 2020, https://www.nytimes.com/2020/10/19/world/asia/china-taiwan-fiji-fight.html.

49. Huileng Tan, "China Holiday Season Starts but Taiwan Tourism Suffering Amid One China Spat," CNBC, September 20, 2016, https://www.cnbc.com/2016/09/16/china-holiday-season-starts-but-taiwan-tourism-suffering-amid-one-china-spat.html; Nick Aspinwall, "Taiwan Promotes 'Freedom Pineapples' in Response to Chinese Import Ban," *The Diplomat*, March 6, 2021, https://thediplomat.com/2021/03/taiwan-promotes-freedom-pineapples-in-response-to-chinese-import-ban; "Chinese Mainland Bars Entry of Meat Products From Taiwan," Xinhua, January 27, 2021, http://www.xinhuanet.com/english/2021-01/27/c_139700988.htm.

50. Huileng Tan, "China Has Banned More Than 2,000 Taiwan Food Imports Amid Pelosi's Visit as Beijing Steps Up Trade Weaponization," *Business Insider*, August 3, 2022, https://www.businessinsider.com/china-bans-thousands-taiwan-food-imports-pelosi-visit-weaponize-trade-2022-8; Grace Zhu, "China Suspends Natural Sand Exports to Taiwan," *Wall Street Journal*, August 2, 2022, https://www.wsj.com/livecoverage/nancy-pelosi-taiwan-visit-china-us-tensions/card/china-suspends-natural-sand-exports-to-taiwan-Jcrk4q1MS8AcVryiBagi.

51. Ben Blanchard, "Choose a Side, China Tells Taiwan Firms as It Punishes Conglomerate," Reuters, November 22, 2022, https://www.reuters.com/markets/commodities/choose-side-china-tells-taiwan-firms-it-punishes-conglomerate-2021-11-22.

52. Liz Lee and Ben Blanchard, "China to Inspect Ships in Taiwan Strait, Taiwan Says Won't Cooperate," Reuters, April 5, 2023, https://www.reuters.com/world/asia-pacific/china-inspect-ships-taiwan-strait-taiwan-says-wont-cooperate-2023-04-06.

53. "General Secretary Xi Jinping Meets With the Joint Visiting Delegation of Taiwan Peaceful Reunification Group," Xinhua, September 26, 2014, http://www.xinhuanet.com//politics/2014-09/26/c_1112641354.htm; "Full Text of Xi Jinping's Report at 19th CPC National Congress," Xinhua, October 18, 2017, http://www.xinhuanet.com/

english/special/2017-11/03/c_136725942.htm; "Xi Says 'China Must Be, Will Be Reunified,' As Key Anniversary Marked," Xinhua, January 2, 2019, http://www. xinhuanet.com/english/2019-01/02/c_137714898.htm. In a meeting with a delegation of groups calling for unification with Taiwan in 2014, Xi Jinping "pointed out that national reunification is a historical necessity for the great rejuvenation of the Chinese nation." In 2019, Xi also stressed that unification was a "must for the great rejuvenation of the Chinese nation."

54. PRC State Council, "Taiwan Question."

55. Xi Jinping, "Hold High the Great Banner of Socialism With Chinese Characteristics and Strive in Unity to Build a Modern Socialist Country in All Respects," report to the Twentieth National Congress of the Communist Party of China, October 16, 2022, https://drive.google.com/file/d/11cnSr-gMAbMv1XF4FzseCIcGL05LhF_k/view.

56. State Council Information Office, "Full Text of Xi Jinping's Speech at First Session of 14th NPC," People's Republic of China, March 15, 2023, http://english.scio.gov.cn/m/topnews/2023-03/15/content_85168965.htm.

57. "Full Text: Speech by Xi Jinping at a Ceremony Marking the Centenary of the CPC," Xinhua, July 1, 2021, http://www.xinhuanet.com/english/special/2021-07/01/c_1310038244.htm; Ben Blanchard, "China's Xi Says Political Solution for Taiwan Can't Wait Forever," Reuters, October 6, 2013, https://www.reuters.com/article/us-asia-apec-china-taiwan/chinas-xi-says-political-solution-for-taiwan-cant-wait-forever-idUSBRE99503Q20131006.

58. MSNBC, "CIA Director Burns 'Wouldn't Underestimate President Xi's Determination' to Control Taiwan," YouTube, July 21, 2022, https://www.youtube.com/watch?v=GXHdQo54gio.

59. Senate Committee on Armed Services, *Hearing to Receive Testimony on Worldwide Threats*, 117th Cong., 82 (2022), https://www.armed-services.senate.gov/imo/media/doc/22-40_05-10-2022.pdf.

60. Antony Blinken, "Secretary Antony J. Blinken With Peggy Collins of Bloomberg News," interview by Peggy Collins, Bloomberg News, October 26, 2022, https://www.state.gov/secretary-antony-j-blinken-with-peggy-collins-of-bloomberg-news.

61. Senate Committee on Armed Services, *Hearing to Receive Testimony on the Posture of United States Indo-Pacific Command and United States Forces Korea*, 117th Cong. 33 (2022), https://www.armed-services.senate.gov/imo/media/doc/22-11_03-10-2022.pdf; Senate Committee on Armed Services, *To Consider the Nomination of Admiral John C. Aquilino, USN, for Reappointment to the Grade of Admiral and to Be Commander, United States Indo-Pacific Command*, 117th Cong. 43 (2021), https://www.armed-services.senate.gov/imo/media/doc/21-14_03-23-2021.pdf.

62. International Monetary Fund, World Economic Outlook Database (for October 2022).

63. Daniel H. Rosen, "China's Economic Reckoning: The Price of Failed Reforms," *Foreign Affairs* 100, no. 4 (July/August 2021), https://www.foreignaffairs.com/articles/china/2021-06-22/chinas-economic-reckoning.

64. Kathrin Hille, "TSMC: How a Taiwanese Chipmaker Became a Linchpin of the Global Economy," *Financial Times*, March 24, 2021, https://www.ft.com/content/05206915-fd73-4a3a-92a5-6760ce965bd9.

65. Chris Miller, *Chip War: The Fight for the World's Most Critical Technology* (New York: Scribner, 2022), 328.

66. General Administration of Customs of the People's Republic of China, 2022, http://stats.customs.gov.cn/indexEn.

67. Organization for Economic Cooperation and Development (OECD), "Measuring Distortions in International Markets: The Semiconductor Value Chain," OECD Trade Policy Paper, no. 234, December 12, 2019, 50, https://doi.org/10.1787/8fe4491d-en.

68. OECD, "Measuring Distortions in International Markets," 84.

69. Shunsuke Tabeta, "'Made in China' Chip Drive Falls Far Short of 70% Self-Sufficiency," *Nikkei Asia*, October 13, 2021, https://asia.nikkei.com/Business/Tech/Semiconductors/Made-in-China-chip-drive-falls-far-short-of-70-self-sufficiency.

70. Edward White and Qianer Liu, "China's Big Fund Corruption Probe Casts Shadow Over Chip Sector," *Financial Times*, September 28, 2022, https://www.ft.com/content/8358e81b-f4e7-4bad-bc08-19a77035e1b4.

71. Alan Crawford, Jarrell Dillard, Helene Fouquet, and Isabel Reynolds, "The World Is Dangerously Dependent on Taiwan for Semiconductors," Bloomberg, January 25, 2021, https://www.bloomberg.com/news/features/2021-01-25/the-world-is-dangerously-dependent-on-taiwan-for-semiconductors; Evelyn Cheng, "China Needs Taiwan's Biggest Chipmaker—More Than the Other Way Around," CNBC, August 19, 2022, https://www.cnbc.com/2022/08/17/china-needs-taiwans-biggest-chipmaker-more-than-the-other-way-around.html.

72. Bureau of Industry and Security, "Commerce Implements New Export Controls on Advanced Computing and Semiconductor Manufacturing Items to the People's Republic of China (PRC)," news release, U.S. Department of Commerce, October 7, 2022, https://www.bis.doc.gov/index.php/documents/about-bis/newsroom/press-releases/3158-2022-10-07-bis-press-release-advanced-computing-and-semiconductor-manufacturing-controls-final/file.

73. Tsai Ing-wen, "Taiwan and the Fight for Democracy: A Force for Good in the Changing International Order," *Foreign Affairs* 111, no. 6 (November/December 2021), https://www.foreignaffairs.com/articles/taiwan/2021-10-05/taiwan-and-fight-democracy.

74. Kathrin Hille and Demetri Sevastopulo, "Warns Europe a Conflict Over Taiwan Could Cause Global Economic Shock," *Financial Times*, November 10, 2022, https://www.ft.com/content/c0b815f3-fd3e-4807-8de7-6b5f72ea8ae5.

75. Deniz Barki and Lucy Deleze-Black, eds., *Review of Maritime Transport, 2016* (Geneva: United Nations Conference on Trade and Development, 2016), https://unctad.org/system/files/official-document/rmt2016_en.pdf.

76. China Power Project, "How Much Trade Transits the South China Sea?," Center for Strategic and International Studies, last modified January 25, 2021, https://chinapower.csis.org/much-trade-transits-south-china-sea.

77. Kevin Varley, "Taiwan Tensions Raise Risks in One of Busiest Shipping Lanes," Bloomberg, August 2, 2022, https://www.bloomberg.com/news/articles/2022-08-02/taiwan-tensions-raise-risks-in-one-of-busiest-shipping-lanes.

78. U.S. Census Bureau, "Trade in Goods With China," accessed April 23, 2023, https://www.census.gov/foreign-trade/balance/c5700.html.

79. CEIC, "Share of International Trade of Goods and Services in Nominal GDP in Taiwan in Selected Quarters From 4th Quarter 2018 to 4th Quarter 2022," Statista, February 27, 2023, https://www.statista.com/statistics/1266254/taiwan-quarterly-trade-to-gdp-ratio.

80. Zhao Ziwen, "China-Taiwan Trade, and Everything You Need to Know," *South China Morning Post*, August 7, 2022, https://www.scmp.com/economy/china-economy/article/3187890/china-taiwan-trade-and-everything-you-need-know.

81. Bonny Lin et al., *Competition in the Gray Zone: Countering China's Coercion Against U.S. Allies and Partners in the Indo-Pacific* (Santa Monica, CA: RAND Corporation, 2022), 51, https://www.rand.org/pubs/research_reports/RRA594-1.html.

82. Miller, *Chip War*, 177.

83. Saheli Roy Choudhury, "Tough Road Ahead for U.S. Firms Trying to Cut Reliance on Taiwan Chipmakers," CNBC, April 13, 2021, https://www.cnbc.com/2021/04/13/semiconductor-shortage-us-tech-companies-and-their-reliance-on-taiwan.html.

84. Miller, *Chip War*, xx.

85. Yuka Hayashi, "Chip Shortage Limits U.S.'s Ability to Supply Weapons to Ukraine, Commerce Secretary Says," *Wall Street Journal*, April 27, 2022, https://www.wsj.com/livecoverage/russia-ukraine-latest-news-2022-04-27/card/chip-shortage-limits-u-s-s-ability-to-supply-weapons-to-ukraine-commerce-secretary-says-pCWERV2HkSPzTdQG4CRI.

86. Charlie Vest, Agatha Kratz, and Reva Goujon, "The Global Economic Disruptions From a Taiwan Conflict," Rhodium Group, December 14, 2022, https://rhg.com/research/taiwan-economic-disruptions.

87. McKinsey and Company, "The CHIPS and Science Act: Here's What's in It," October 4, 2022, https://www.mckinsey.com/industries/public-and-social-sector/our-insights/the-chips-and-science-act-heres-whats-in-it.

88. Don Clark and Ana Swanson, "U.S. Pours Money Into Chips, but Even Soaring Spending Has Limits," *New York Times*, January 1, 2023, https://www.nytimes.com/2023/01/01/technology/us-chip-making-china-invest.html.

89. TSMC, "TSMC Announces Updates for TSMC Arizona," press release, December 6, 2022, https://pr.tsmc.com/english/news/2977https://pr.tsmc.com/english/news/2977.

90. John VerWey, "No Permits, No Fabs: The Importance of Regulatory Reform for Semiconductor Manufacturing," Center for Security and Emerging Technology, October 2021, https://cset.georgetown.edu/publication/no-permits-no-fabs; Clark and Swanson, "U.S. Pours Money Into Chips."

91. Tim Culpan, "Sorry, USA, $40 Billion Won't Buy Chip Independence," Bloomberg, December 7, 2022, https://www.bloomberg.com/opinion/articles/2022-12-07/-40-billion-us-semiconductor-plant-won-t-buy-independence.

92. Zongyuan Zoe Liu, "China Is Hardening Itself for Economic War," *Foreign Policy*, June 16, 2022, https://foreignpolicy.com/2022/06/16/china-economic-war-decoupling-united-states-containment.

93. Jude Blanchette and Andrew Polk, "Dual Circulation and China's New Hedged Integration Strategy," Center for Strategic and International Studies, August 24, 2020, https://www.csis.org/analysis/dual-circulation-and-chinas-new-hedged-integration-strategy.

94. Tai Ming Cheung, Barry Naughton, and Eric Hagt, *China's Roadmap to Becoming a Science, Technology, and Innovation Great Power in the 2020s and Beyond: Assessing Its Medium- and Long-Term Strategies and Plans* (La Jolla, CA: UC Institute on Global Conflict and Cooperation, July 2022), 9, https://ucigcc.org/wp-content/uploads/2022/07/Ocea-revised-19-July-2022-1.pdf.

95. State Council, "Full Text: Resolution of the CPC Central Committee on the Major Achievements and Historical Experience of the Party Over the Past Century," news release, People's Republic of China, November 16, 2021, https://english.www.gov.cn/policies/latestreleases/202111/16/content_WS6193a935c6d0df57f98e50b0.html.

96. National People's Congress of the People's Republic of China, "Export Control Law of the People's Republic of China," October 17, 2020, http://www.npc.gov.cn/englishnpc/c23934/202112/63aff482fece44a591b45810fa2c25c4.shtml.

97. National People's Congress of the People's Republic of China, "Anti-Foreign Sanctions Law of the People's Republic of China," June 10, 2021, http://www.npc.gov.cn/npc/c30834/202106/d4a714d5813c4ad2ac54a5f0f78a5270.shtml.

98. *The Future of U.S. Policy on Taiwan, Before the Senate Comm. on Foreign Relations*, 117th Cong. (2021) (testimony of Ely Ratner, assistant secretary of defense for Indo-Pacific security affairs, U.S. Department of Defense), https://www.foreign.senate.gov/imo/media/doc/120821_Ratner_Testimony1.pdf.

99. Brendan Rittenhouse and Caitlin Talmadge, "The Consequences of Conquest: Why Indo-Pacific Power Hinges on Taiwan," *Foreign Affairs* 101, no. 4 (July/August 2022), https://www.foreignaffairs.com/articles/china/2022-06-16/consequences-conquest-taiwan-indo-pacific.

100. Hille and Sevastopulo, "US Warns Europe."; Charlie Vest, Agatha Kratz, and Reva Goujon, "The Global Economic Disruptions from a Taiwan Conflict," *Rhodium Group*, December 14, 2022, https://rhg.com/research/taiwan-economic-disruptions.

101. Ian Vásquez, Fred McMahon, Ryan Murphy, and Guillermina Sutter Schneider, *The Human Freedom Index 2022: A Global Measurement of Personal, Civil, and Economic Freedom* (Washington, DC, and Vancouver: Cato Institute and Fraser Institute, 2022), https://www.fraserinstitute.org/sites/default/files/human-freedom-index-2022.pdf.

102. *PLA Operational Concepts and Centers of Gravity in a Taiwan Conflict, Before the U.S.-China Economic and Security Review Commission*, 117th Cong. (2021) (testimony of Lonnie Henley, professional lecturer, George Washington University), https://www.uscc.gov/sites/default/files/2021-02/Lonnie_Henley_Testimony.pdf.

103. China Power Project, "What Does China Really Spend on Its Military?," Center for Strategic and International Studies, last modified June 29, 2022, https://chinapower.csis.org/military-spending.

104. U.S. Department of Defense, *Military and Security Developments Involving the People's Republic of China, 2021: Annual Report to Congress* (Washington, DC: Office of the Secretary of Defense, 2021), 142, https://media.defense.gov/2021/Nov/03/

2002885874/-1/-1/0/2021-CMPR-FINAL.PDF. For more on this, see Nan Tian and Fei Su, *A New Estimate of China's Military Expenditure* (Solna, Sweden: Stockholm International Peace Research Institute, 2021), https://www.sipri.org/sites/default/files/2021-01/2101_sipri_report_a_new_estimate_of_chinas_military_expenditure.pdf.

105. Lisa Ferdinando, "DoD Officials: Chinese Actions Threaten U.S. Technological, Industrial Base," news release, U.S. Department of Defense, June 21, 2018, https://www.defense.gov/News/News-Stories/Article/Article/1557188/dod-officials-chinese-actions-threaten-us-technological-industrial-base; Jeffrey B. Jones, "Confronting China's Efforts to Steal Defense Information," Belfer Center for Science and International Affairs, May 2020, https://www.belfercenter.org/publication/confronting-chinas-efforts-steal-defense-information.

106. U.S. Department of Defense, *Military and Security Developments Involving the People's Republic of China, 2022* (Washington, DC: Office of the Secretary of Defense, 2022), https://media.defense.gov/2022/Nov/29/2003122279/-1/-1/1/2022-MILITARY-AND-SECURITY-DEVELOPMENTS-INVOLVING-THE-PEOPLES-REPUBLIC-OF-CHINA.PDF.

107. U.S. Department of Defense, *Military and Security Developments, 2022*, 49.

108. U.S. Department of Defense, *Military and Security Developments, 2022*.

109. For more on this, see Abraham Denmark and Caitlin Talmadge, "Why China Wants More and Better Nukes," *Foreign Affairs*, November 19, 2021, https://www.foreignaffairs.com/articles/china/2021-11-19/why-china-wants-more-and-better-nukes.

110. U.S. Department of Defense, *Military and Security Developments*, 2022.

111. Michael R. Gordon, "China Has More ICBM Launchers Than U.S., American Military Reports," *Wall Street Journal*, February 7, 2023, https://www.wsj.com/articles/china-has-more-icbm-launchers-than-u-s-american-military-reports-11675779463.

112. Senate Armed Forces Subcommittee on Strategic Forces, *Hearing to Receive Testimony on the Nuclear Weapons Council,* 117th Cong. 11 (2022), https://www.armed-services.senate.gov/imo/media/doc/22-37_05-04-2022.pdf.

113. Notwithstanding this reticence, some deviations from the policy have occurred over the years. For instance, President George W. Bush in 2001 was asked if the United States had an obligation to defend Taiwan against a PRC attack and responded, "Yes, we do." When asked if that would entail the full force of the American military, Bush replied, "Whatever it took to help Taiwan defend herself." His administration, however, quickly clarified that his comments did not represent any change in policy. "Bush Vows Taiwan Support," ABC News, April 25, 2001, https://abcnews.go.com/US/story?id=93471&page=1.

114. For a brief debate on the merits of strategic ambiguity, see Bonnie S. Glaser, Michael J. Mazarr, Michael J. Glennon, Richard Haass, and David Sacks, "Should American Support for Taiwan Be Ambiguous?," *Foreign Affairs*, September 24, 2020, https://www.foreignaffairs.com/articles/united-states/2020-09-24/dire-straits.

115. Richard Haass and David Sacks, "American Support for Taiwan Must Be Unambiguous," *Foreign Affairs*, September 2, 2020, https://www.foreignaffairs.com/articles/united-states/american-support-taiwan-must-be-unambiguous.

116. Ivan Kanapathy, "Taiwan Doesn't Need a Formal U.S. Security Guarantee," *Foreign Policy*, April 26, 2022, https://foreignpolicy.com/2022/04/26/taiwan-us-security-guarantee-defense-china-ukraine-war; Glaser et al., "Should American Support for Taiwan Be Ambiguous?"

117. Cancian et al., *First Battle of the Next War.*

118. U.S. Department of Defense, "Secretary of Defense Lloyd J. Austin III and Army General Mark A. Milley, Chairman, Joint Chiefs of Staff, Hold a Press Briefing Following Ukrainian Defense Contact Group Meeting," transcript, November 16, 2022, https://www.defense.gov/News/Transcripts/Transcript/Article/3220910/secretary-of-defense-lloyd-j-austin-iii-and-army-general-mark-a-milley-chairman.

119. Joel Wuthnow et al., eds., *Crossing the Strait: China's Military Prepares for War With Taiwan* (Washington, DC: National Defense University Press, 2022), 23.

120. Kevin McCauley, *China Maritime Report No. 22: Logistics Support for a Cross-Strait Invasion—The View From Beijing* (Newport, RI: U.S. Naval War College China Maritime Studies Institute, 2022), https://digital-commons.usnwc.edu/cgi/viewcontent.cgi?article=1021&context=cmsi-maritime-reports.

121. *PLA Operational Concepts and Centers of Gravity in a Taiwan Conflict* (testimony of Lonnie Henley).

122. Michael Martina and David Brunnstrom, "CIA Chief Warns Against Underestimating Xi's Ambitions Toward Taiwan," Reuters, February 2, 2023, https://www.reuters.com/world/cia-chief-says-chinas-xi-little-sobered-by-ukraine-war-2023-02-02.

123. U.S. Department of Defense, *Military and Security Developments, 2022.*

124. Senate Committee on Armed Services, *Hearing to Receive Testimony on United States Indo-Pacific Command in Review of the Defense Authorization Request for Fiscal Year 2022 and the Future Years Defense Program*, 117th Cong. 48 (2021), https://www.armed-services.senate.gov/imo/media/doc/21-10_03-09-2021.pdf.

125. Mikio Sugeno and Tsuyoshi Nagasawa, "Xi's Potential 2027 Transition Poses Threat to Taiwan: Davidson," Nikkei Asia, September 18, 2021, https://asia.nikkei.com/Editor-s-Picks/Interview/Xi-s-potential-2027-transition-poses-threat-to-Taiwan-Davidson.

126. Lawrence Chung, "Beijing 'Fully Able' to Invade Taiwan by 2025, Island's Defence Minister Says," *South China Morning Post*, October 6, 2021, https://www.scmp.com/news/china/military/article/3151340/beijing-capable-taiwan-invasion-2025-islands-defence-minister.

127. Thomas Shugart, "Mind the Gap: How China's Civilian Shipping Could Enable a Taiwan Invasion," War on the Rocks, August 16, 2021, https://warontherocks.com/2021/08/mind-the-gap-how-chinas-civilian-shipping-could-enable-a-taiwan-invasion.

128. U.S. Department of Defense, *Military and Security Developments, 2022*; J. Michael Dahm, *China Maritime Report No. 16: Chinese Ferry Tales—The PLA's Use of Civilian Shipping in Support of Over-the-Shore Logistics* (Newport, RI: U.S. Naval War College China Maritime Studies Institute, 2021), https://digital-commons.usnwc.edu/cgi/viewcontent.cgi?article=1015&context=cmsi-maritime-reports.

129. Lonnie D. Henley, *China Maritime Report No. 21: Civilian Shipping and Maritime Militia—The Logistics Backbone of a Taiwan Invasion* (Newport, RI: U.S. Naval War College China Maritime Studies Institute, 2022), https://digital-commons.usnwc.edu/cgi/viewcontent.cgi?article=1020&context=cmsi-maritime-reports.

130. National People's Congress of the People's Republic of China, "Reserve Services Personnel Law of the People's Republic of China," December 30, 2022, http://www.npc.gov.cn/npc/c30834/202212/675bfdf572d1440d89e29080e7310b6f.shtml.

131. National People's Congress of the People's Republic of China, "中华人民共和国立法法 [People's Republic of China's Legislation Law]," March 4, 2023, http://www.npc.gov.cn/npc/kgfb/202303/eb5e0e60ff5f43f7a3bfa2a10bbee6ba.shtml.

132. U.S. Department of Defense, *Military and Security Developments, 2022.*

133. "Explainer: Prudent Chinese Defense Budget Growth Ensures Broad Public Security," Xinhua, March 5, 2022, https://english.news.cn/20220305/e044f80401f5401daa8a188d7eed7a55/c.html; Yimou Lee and Ben Blanchard, "Taiwan Aims for Big Rise in Defence Spending Amid Escalating China Tension," Reuters, August 25, 2022, https://www.reuters.com/business/aerospace-defense/taiwan-proposes-129-on-year-rise-defence-spending-2023-2022-08-25.

134. Helen Davidson, "Taiwan's Military Recruitment Pool Shrinking Due to Low Birthrate," *The Guardian*, October 4, 2022, https://www.theguardian.com/world/2022/oct/04/taiwan-military-recruitment-low-birthrate-chinese-invasion-threat.

135. Ian Easton, Mark Stokes, Cortez A. Cooper III, and Arthur Chan, *Transformation of Taiwan's Reserve Force* (Washington, DC: RAND Corporation, 2017), https://www.rand.org/pubs/research_reports/RR1757.html.

136. Joel Wuthnow et al., eds., *Crossing the Strait*, 6.

137. Lee Hsi-min and Eric Lee, "Taiwan's Overall Defense Concept, Explained," *The Diplomat*, November 3, 2020, https://thediplomat.com/2020/11/taiwans-overall-defense-concept-explained; Drew Thompson, "Winning the Fight Taiwan Cannot Afford to Lose," *Strategic Forum* 310 (October 2021), https://ndupress.ndu.edu/Media/News/Article/2833298/winning-the-fight-taiwan-cannot-afford-to-lose.

138. Kathrin Hille, "China Pressure Deepens Taiwan's Desire for Big US Weapons Systems," *Financial Times*, August 18, 2022, https://www.ft.com/content/0d492ad7-9346-4c9e-b186-834c6fc75e85.

139. Jeanny Kao and Yimou Lee, "Taiwan to Boost Energy Inventories Amid China Threat," Reuters, October 23, 2022, https://www.reuters.com/business/energy/taiwan-boost-energy-inventories-amid-china-threat-2022-10-24.

140. Council of Agriculture, "Comprehensive Grain Self-sufficiency Rate," Republic of China (Taiwan) Executive Yuan, accessed April 23, 2023, https://statview.coa.gov.tw/aqsys_on/importantArgiGoal_lv3_1_5_1.html; "Taiwan Targets 40% Food Self-Sufficiency Rate by 2020," Focus Taiwan, May 11, 2011, https://focustaiwan.tw/business/201105110022.

141. Statistics Database Query, "Total Imports/Total Exports," Republic of China (Taiwan) Ministry of Finance, accessed April 23, 2023, https://portal.sw.nat.gov.tw/APGA/GA30E; Raymond Cheng, "Medicines Shortage Spreads Overseas as People Buy Panadol to Send to China," Radio Free Asia, December 19, 2022, https://www.rfa.org/english/news/china/shortage-12192022135536.html.

142. Statistics Database Query, "Total Imports/Total Exports."

143. Lee and Blanchard, "Taiwan Aims for Big Rise."

144. Kathrin Hille, "Taiwan Rallies Drone Makers to Prepare Military for China Threat," *Financial Times*, November 8, 2022, https://www.ft.com/content/ec221278-127e-40d4-859e-9f2408bf3f7e; Matt Yu and Sean Lin, "Missile Production to More Than Double With Completion of New Facilities," Focus Taiwan, August 13, 2022, https://focustaiwan.tw/sci-tech/202208130014.

145. Office of the President of the Republic of China (Taiwan), "President Tsai Announces Military Force Realignment Plan," news release, December 27, 2022, https://english.president.gov.tw/NEWS/6417.

146. Joseph Yeh, "Ukraine Example Helps NGO Civil Defense Programs Grain Traction," Focus Taiwan, March 11, 2023, https://focustaiwan.tw/politics/202303110007; Chen Yu-fu, "Robert Tsao Pledges Money to Make 1m Combat Drones," *Taipei Times*, September 24, 2022, https://www.taipeitimes.com/News/taiwan/archives/2022/09/24/2003785860.

147. Russell Hsiao, "The Ukraine War and Its Impact on Taiwanese Perceptions on Defense Issues," Global Taiwan Institute, May 4, 2022, https://globaltaiwan.org/2022/05/the-ukraine-war-and-its-impact-on-taiwanese-perceptions-on-defense-issues.

148. Eric Heginbotham et al., *The U.S.-China Military Scorecard: Forces, Geography, and the Evolving Balance of Power, 1996–2017* (Santa Monica, CA: RAND Corporation, 2015), 54.

149. *Deterring PRC Aggression Toward Taiwan, Before the U.S.-China Economic and Security Review Commission*, 117th Cong. (2021) (statement of Thomas Shugart, adjunct senior fellow, Center for a New American Security), https://www.uscc.gov/sites/default/files/2021- 02/Thomas_Shugart_Testimony.pdf.

150. Eric Heginbotham et al., *U.S.-China Military Scorecard*.

151. Cancian et al., *First Battle of the Next War*.

152. U.S. Department of Defense, "2022 National Defense Strategy of the United States of America," October 2022, https://media.defense.gov/2022/Oct/27/2003103845/-1/-1/1/2022-NATIONAL-DEFENSE-STRATEGY-NPR-MDR.PDF.

153. *Future of U.S. Policy on Taiwan* (testimony of Ely Ratner).

154. For more on this undertaking, see U.S. Marine Corps, "Force Design 2030," accessed April 23, 2023 https://www.marines.mil/Force-Design-2030.

155. Hibbah Kaileh and Luke A. Nicastro, "The Pacific Deterrence Initiative: A Budgetary Overview," Congressional Research Service, January 9, 2023, https://sgp.fas.org/crs/natsec/IF12303.pdf.

156. Bryant Harris, "Pacific Forces Wish List Seeks $3.5 Billion More Than Biden Budget," *Defense News*, March 24, 2023, https://www.defensenews.com/congress/budget/2023/03/24/pacific-forces-wish-list-seeks-35-billion-more-than-biden-budget.

157. John Ismay and Thomas Gibbons-Neff, "Artillery Is Breaking in Ukraine. It's Becoming a Problem for the Pentagon," *New York Times*, November 25, 2022, https://www.nytimes.com/2022/11/25/us/ukraine-artillery-breakdown.html.

158. Bryan Bender and Lara Seligman, "'We Haven't Got This Figured Out Just Yet': Pentagon, Industry Struggle to Arm Ukraine," *Politico*, December 4, 2022, https://www.politico.com/news/2022/12/04/pentagon-industry-struggle-to-arm-ukraine-00072125.

159. For more on Japan's potential role and contributions, see David Sacks, *Enhancing U.S.-Japan Coordination for a Taiwan Conflict* (New York: Council on Foreign Relations, 2022), https://www.cfr.org/report/enhancing-us-japan-coordination-taiwan-conflict.

160. White House, "U.S.-Japan Joint Leaders' Statement: 'U.S.-Japan Global Partnership for a New Era,'" April 16, 2021, https://www.whitehouse.gov/briefing-room/statements-releases/2021/04/16/u-s-japan-joint-leaders-statement-u-s-japan-global-partnership-for-a-new-era.

161. Ben Blanchard, "Former PM Abe Says Japan, U.S. Could Not Stand by if China Attacked Taiwan," Reuters, November 30, 2021, https://www.reuters.com/world/asia-pacific/former-pm-abe-says-japan-us-could-not-stand-by-if-china-attacked-taiwan-2021-12-01.

162. Peter Landers, "Japan Prime Minister Contender Takes Harder Line on Missile-Strike Ability," *Wall Street Journal*, September 7, 2021, https://www.wsj.com/articles/contender-for-japan-leader-sees-need-for-missile-strike-ability-11631015401.

163. Kylie MacLellan, "Ukraine Plight Could Be Replicated in East Asia, Japan's Kishida Warns," Reuters, May 6, 2022, https://www.reuters.com/world/asia-pacific/peace-stability-taiwan-strait-is-critical-japanese-pm-2022-05-05.

164. Office of the President of Ukraine, "Joint Statement on Special Global Partnership Between Ukraine and Japan," March 21, 2023, https://www.president.gov.ua/en/news/spilna-zayava-pro-osoblive-globalne-partnerstvo-mizh-ukrayin-81717.

165. Cabinet Secretariat of Japan, "National Security Strategy of Japan," December 2022, https://www.cas.go.jp/jp/siryou/221216anzenhoshou/nss-e.pdf.

166. U.S. Department of State, "Joint Statement of the Security Consultative Committee ('2+2')," January 11, 2023, https://www.state.gov/joint-statement-of-the-security-consultative-committee-22.

167. Lidia Kelly, "'Inconceivable' Australia Would Not Join U.S. to Defend Taiwan—Australian Defence Minister," Reuters, November 12, 2021, https://www.reuters.com/world/asia-pacific/inconceivable-australia-would-not-join-us-defend-taiwan-australian-defence-2021-11-12. Although Australia's Defense Minister noted in March 2023 that Canberra did not commit to supporting the United States during a conflict over Taiwan in exchange for access to submarines, that statement only addressed a narrow question on the parameters of the AUKUS arrangement rather than Australia's strategic interests and decisions. Sam McKeith, "Australia Did Not Vow to Help U.S. Defend Taiwan in Submarine Deal, Minister Says," Reuters, March 18, 2023, https://www.reuters.com/world/australia-did-not-promise-us-support-taiwan-submarines-deal-2023-03-19.

168. Natasha Kassam, "Lowy Institute Poll 2022," June 29, 2022, https://poll.lowyinstitute.org/charts/war-over-taiwan.

169. White House, "Readout of President Joe Biden's Meeting With Prime Minister Anthony Albanese of Australia," November 13, 2022, https://www.whitehouse.gov/briefing-room/statements-releases/2022/11/13/readout-of-president-joe-bidens-meeting-with-prime-minister-anthony-albanese-of-australia.

170. U.S. Department of State, "Joint Statement on Australia-U.S. Ministerial Consultations (AUSMIN) 2022," December 6, 2022, https://www.state.gov/joint-statement-on-australia-u-s-ministerial-consultations-ausmin-2022.

171. Office of the Deputy Prime Minister of Australia, "Australia Welcomes United Sates Marines Back to Darwin," March 22, 2023, https://www.pacom.mil/Media/News/News-Article-View/Article/3338043/australia-welcomes-united-sates-marines-back-to-darwin.

172. Xave Gregorio, "Manalo: Philippines Won't Let US Store Weapons for Taiwan Ops at EDCA Sites," *Philippine Star*, April 19, 2023, https://www.philstar.com/headlines/2023/04/19/2260092/manalo-philippines-wont-let-us-store-weapons-taiwan-ops-edca-sites.

173. "Transcript: Philippine President Marcos Speaks With Nikkei Asia," *Nikkei Asia*, February 13, 2023, https://asia.nikkei.com/Editor-s-Picks/Interview/Transcript-Philippine-President-Marcos-speaks-with-Nikkei-Asia.

174. White House, "Joint Statement of the Leaders of the United States and the Philippines," May 1, 2023, https://www.whitehouse.gov/briefing-room/statements-releases/2023/05/01/joint-statement-of-the-leaders-of-the-united-states-and-the-philippines.

175. Michael Martina, Don Durfee, and David Brunnstrom, "Marcos Says Philippines Bases Could Be 'Useful' if Taiwan Attacked," Reuters, May 5, 2023, https://www.reuters.com/world/asia-pacific/marcos-says-philippines-bases-could-be-useful-if-taiwan-attacked-2023-05-05/.

176. Blanchard, "U.S. Should Recognize Taiwan."

177. Anti-Secession Law (adopted at the third session of the tenth National People's Congress on March 14, 2005), https://www.europarl.europa.eu/meetdocs/2004_2009/documents/fd/d-cn2005042601/d-cn2005042601en.pdf.

178. Taiwan Relations Act, H.R. 2479, 96th Cong. (1979).

179. Dina Smeltz and Craig Kafura, "Americans Favor Aiding Taiwan With Arms but Not Troops," Chicago Council on Global Affairs, August 2022, https://globalaffairs.org/sites/default/files/2022-08/2022%20CCS%20Taiwan%20Brief.pdf.

180. Louise Watt, "Taiwan Says It Tried to Warn the World About Coronavirus. Here's What It Really Knew and When," *Time*, May 19, 2020, https://time.com/5826025/taiwan-who-trump-coronavirus-covid19.

181. Open Doors, "All Places of Origin," accessed April 23, 2023, https://opendoorsdata.org/data/international-students/all-places-of-origin; Open Doors, "All Destinations," accessed April 23, 2023, https://opendoorsdata.org/data/us-study-abroad/all-destinations.

182. American Institute in Taiwan, "Fact Sheet on U.S.-Taiwan Education Initiative," December 3, 2020, https://www.ait.org.tw/fact-sheet-on-u-s-taiwan-education-initiative.

183. Taiwan Bureau of Trade, "Trade Statistics," Ministry of Economic Affairs, Republic of China (Taiwan), accessed April 23, 2023, https://cuswebo.trade.gov.tw/FSCE000F/FSCE000F.

184. Office of the United States Trade Representative, "United States and Taiwan Announce the Launch of the U.S.-Taiwan Initiative on 21st-Century Trade," June 1, 2022, https://ustr.gov/about-us/policy-offices/press-office/press-releases/2022/june/united-states-and-taiwan-announce-launch-us-taiwan-initiative-21st-century-trade.

185. In 2019, for instance, 161 members of the U.S. House of Representatives signed a letter calling for the United States to pursue a trade deal with Taiwan. Letter to U.S. Trade Representative Robert E. Lighthizer, December 19, 2019, https://mariodiazbalart.house.gov/sites/evo-subsites/mariodiazbalart.house.gov/files/wysiwyg_uploaded/12.19.19%20CTC%20Letter%20re.%20Taiwan%20FTA_.pdf. The following year, a bipartisan group of fifty senators signed a similar letter. U.S. Senate Foreign Relations Committee, "Risch, Inhofe, Menendez, Colleagues Urge Lighthizer to Begin Talks for a Trade Agreement With Taiwan," press release, October 1, 2020, https://www.foreign.senate.gov/press/rep/release/risch-inhofe-menendez-colleagues-urge-lighthizer-to-begin-talks-for-a-trade-agreement-with-taiwan.

186. Office of United States Trade Representative, *2021 National Trade Estimate Report on Foreign Trade Barriers*, 2021, https://ustr.gov/sites/default/files/files/reports/2021/2021NTE.pdf.

187. International Trade Administration, "Taiwan—Country Commercial Guide," U.S. Department of Commerce, September 15, 2022, https://www.trade.gov/country-commercial-guides/taiwan-market-overview.

188. Lara Seligman, "China Dominates the Rare Earths Market. This U.S. Mine Is Trying to Change That.," *Politico Magazine*, December 14, 2022, https://www.politico.com/news/magazine/2022/12/14/rare-earth-mines-00071102.

189. Rodrigo Castillo and Caitlin Purdy, *China's Role in Supplying Critical Minerals for the Global Energy Transition: What Could the Future Hold?* (Washington, DC: Brookings Institution, July 2022), https://www.brookings.edu/wp-content/uploads/2022/08/LTRC_ChinaSupplyChain.pdf.

190. Anna Nishino et al., "The Great Medicines Migration: How China Took Control of Key Global Pharmaceutical Supplies," *Nikkei Asia*, April 5, 2022, https://asia.nikkei.com/static/vdata/infographics/chinavaccine-3/.

191. In 2016, for instance, after President Tsai did not endorse the 1992 Consensus, Taiwanese tourism plummeted by 22 percent. In 2019, Taiwanese beverage chains were forced to adopt Chinese claims over Taiwan and Hong Kong, and in 2021 China banned the import of Taiwanese pineapples. In 2022, China blocked the export of natural sand to Taiwan following Speaker Pelosi's visit and banned a list of Taiwanese products.

192. World Integrated Trade Solution, "China Trade Summary 2020," accessed February 17, 2023, https://wits.worldbank.org/CountryProfile/en/Country/CHN/Year/2020/SummaryText.

193. Tim McDonald, "China and Taiwan Face Off in Pineapple War," BBC, March 19, 2021, https://www.bbc.com/news/business-56353963.

194. "Export of Fresh Pineapple From Taiwan," Tridge, accessed April 23, 2023, https://www.tridge.com/intelligences/pineapple/TW/export.

195. Taiwan Relations Act, H.R. 2479, 96th Cong. (1979).

196. U.S. Defense Security Cooperation Agency, "Historical Sales Book: Fiscal Year 1950–2022," accessed April 23, 2023, https://www.dsca.mil/sites/default/files/2023-01/FY%202022%20Historical%20Sales%20Book.pdf.

197. This discussion draws on Sacks, *Enhancing U.S.-Japan Coordination.*

198. Seth G. Jones, *Empty Bins in a Wartime Environment: The Challenge to the U.S. Defense Industrial Base* (Washington, DC: Center for Strategic and International Studies, 2023).

199. James M. Inhofe National Defense Authorization Act for Fiscal Year 2023, Pub. L. No. 117–263 (2022), https://www.congress.gov/bill/117th-congress/house-bill/7776/text.

200. Cancian et al., *First Battle of the Next War.*

201. Megan Eckstein, "Submarine Maintenance Backlogs and Delays Take Toll on Fleet's Development Work at Sea," *Defense News,* February 16, 2022, https://www.defensenews.com/naval/2022/02/16/submarine-maintenance-backlogs-and-delays-take-toll-on-fleets-development-work-at-sea.

202. U.S. Navy Office of Information, "Seismic Mitigation Work on Two Pacific Northwest Dry Docks Begins," February 15, 2023, https://www.navy.mil/Press-Office/News-Stories/Article/3280857/navy-to-temporarily-suspend-some-dry-dock-operations-in-the-pacific-northwest.

203. Gordon Lubold, Doug Cameron, and Nancy A. Youssef, "U.S. Effort to Arm Taiwan Faces New Challenge With Ukraine Conflict," *Wall Street Journal,* November 27, 2022, https://www.wsj.com/articles/u-s-effort-to-arm-taiwan-faces-new-challenge-with-ukraine-conflict-11669559116.

204. Eric Lipton, "From Rockets to Ball Bearings, Pentagon Struggles to Feed War Machine," *New York Times,* March 24, 2023, https://www.nytimes.com/2023/03/24/us/politics/military-weapons-ukraine-war.html.

205. Alastair Iain Johnston, Tsai Chia-hung, and George Yin, "When Might US Political Support Be Unwelcome in Taiwan?," Brookings Institution, April 5, 2023, https://www.brookings.edu/blog/order-from-chaos/2023/04/05/when-might-us-political-support-be-unwelcome-in-taiwan/.

ACRONYMS

ADIZ
air defense identification zone

AIT
American Institute in Taiwan

API
active pharmaceutical ingredient

ASW
anti-submarine warfare

AUKUS
trilateral security agreement
between Australia, the United
Kingdom, and the United States

BIS
U.S. Department of Commerce
Bureau of Industry and Security

BTA
bilateral trade agreement

CCP
Chinese Communist Party

CHIPS and Science Act
Creating Helpful Incentives to
Produce Semiconductors and
Science Act

CPTPP
Comprehensive and
Progressive Agreement for
Trans-Pacific Partnership

C4ISR
Command, Control,
Communications, Computers,
Intelligence, Surveillance, and
Reconnaissance

DPP
Democratic Progressive Party

DOD
U.S. Department of Defense

FMS
foreign military sales

FY
fiscal year

GCTF
Global Cooperation and
Training Framework

GDP
gross domestic product

GMLRS
guided multiple launch
rocket system

HIMARS
high mobility artillery
rocket system

ICAO
International Civil
Aviation Organization

ICT
information and
communications technology

INDOPACOM
U.S. Indo-Pacific Command

Interpol
International Criminal
Police Organization

IPEC
Indo-Pacific Economic Coalition

IPEF
Indo-Pacific Economic
Framework

ISN
U.S. Department of State Bureau
of International Security and
Nonproliferation

ISR
intelligence, surveillance,
and reconnaissance

KMT
Kuomintang

NDAA
National Defense
Authorization Act

ODC
Overall Defense Concept

PDI
Pacific Deterrence Initiative

PLA
People's Liberation Army

PLAN
People's Liberation Army Navy

PRC
People's Republic of China

RCEP
Regional Comprehensive
Economic Partnership

RIMPAC
Rim of the Pacific

RMB
renminbi (Chinese currency)

ROC
Republic of China (Taiwan)

SMIC
Semiconductor Manufacturing
International Corporation

TSMC
Taiwan Semiconductor
Manufacturing Company

TRA
U.S. Taiwan Relations Act

UNCTAD
United Nations Conference on
Trade and Development

USMCA
United States-Mexico-Canada
Agreement

USTR
U.S. Trade Representative

WHO
World Health Organization

TASK FORCE MEMBERS

Task Force members are asked to join a consensus signifying that they endorse "the general policy thrust and judgments reached by the group, though not necessarily every finding and recommendation." They participate in the Task Force in their individual, not institutional, capacities.

Kevin M. Brown is the executive vice president of global operations and chief supply chain officer for Dell Technologies, where he leads an organization of approximately 7,700 team members in twenty-three countries, with a procurement budget of $76 billion. During his two decades at Dell, he has held leadership positions in several business units, including chief procurement officer, along with earlier positions setting up lean manufacturing organizations in the United States and Malaysia. Prior to working at Dell, Brown spent ten years in the shipbuilding industry, working on U.S. Department of Defense projects. He serves on the board of directors for Kroger, the Congressional Black Caucus Foundation, and the Howard University Center for Supply Chain Excellence. Brown is a member of the Executive Leadership Council and the George Washington University National Advisory Council. He earned a BS in mechanical engineering from the University of Massachusetts Amherst and an MS in engineering management from George Washington University.

Michèle A. Flournoy is the cofounder and managing partner of West-Exec Advisors. She served as the undersecretary of defense for policy at the U.S. Department of Defense from 2009 to 2012, and co-led President Barack Obama's transition at the Defense Department. In 2007, Flournoy cofounded the Center for a New American Security (CNAS), where she served as president from 2007 to 2009 and as chief executive officer from 2014 to 2017. Previously, she was senior advisor at the Center for Strategic and International Studies for several years and, prior to that role, a distinguished research professor at the Institute for National Strategic Studies at the National Defense University. Flournoy also served as principal deputy assistant secretary of defense for strategy and threat reduction and deputy assistant secretary of defense for strategy at the U.S. Department of Defense. She serves on the boards of CNAS (where she is the chair), Booz Allen Hamilton, Astra, Amida Technology Solutions, America's Frontier Fund, the Gates Global Policy Center, the War Horse, and CARE. Flournoy is a senior fellow at Harvard's Belfer Center for Science and International Affairs, a distinguished professor of the practice at Georgia Tech's Nunn School of International Affairs, and a member of the Defense Policy Board. She earned a bachelor's degree from Harvard University and a master's degree from Balliol College, Oxford University.

Susan M. Gordon is the founder and principal of GordonVentures LLC, a consultancy focused on technology and global risk. Between 2017 and 2019, she served as the principal deputy director of national intelligence at the Office of the Director of National Intelligence. Prior to that role, Gordon was deputy director of the National Geospatial-Intelligence Agency (NGA) from 2015 to 2017. She served for decades as a career intelligence officer in the Central Intelligence Agency and the NGA. Gordon also serves as a senior fellow at Harvard University; an independent director at CACI International, BlackSky, and SecurityScorecard; a trustee at the MITRE Corporation; an advisor to Microsoft and other technology companies; and a member of the Defense Innovation Board.

Harry Harris served as U.S. ambassador to South Korea from 2018 to 2021. Prior to that post, he served forty years in the U.S. Navy, culminating as commander of the U.S. Indo-Pacific Command from 2015 to 2018, when he retired. He previously commanded the U.S. Pacific Fleet, U.S. 6th Fleet, Striking and Support Forces NATO, Joint Task Force Guantanamo, Patrol and Reconnaissance Wing 1, and Patrol Squadron 46. He participated in Operations Attain Document, Desert Shield/Storm, Southern Watch, Enduring Freedom, Iraqi Freedom, Willing Spirit, and Odyssey Dawn. Between 2011 and 2013, Harris was assistant to the chairman of the Joint Chiefs of Staff, where he was the direct representative of the chairman to Secretaries of State Hillary Clinton and John Kerry. He is the recipient of the State Department's Distinguished Honor Award, the CIA's Agency Seal Medal and Ambassador's Award, the Republic of Korea's Tong-il Order of National Security Merit and Gwanghwa Order of Diplomatic Service Merit, Japan's Grand Cordon of the Rising Sun, the Order of Australia, Tufts University's Dr. Jean Mayer Global Citizenship Award, and numerous other honors. Harris holds degrees from the U.S. Naval Academy, Harvard Kennedy School, and Georgetown University.

Paul Heer is a nonresident senior fellow at the Chicago Council on Global Affairs. Between 2007 and 2015, he served as the national intelligence officer for East Asia in the Office of the Director of National Intelligence (ODNI). Prior to that role, Heer was an East Asian affairs analyst at the Central Intelligence Agency for three decades. He is a recipient of the CIA's Distinguished Career Intelligence Medal and the ODNI's National Intelligence Distinguished Service Medal. From 1999 to 2000, Heer was an intelligence fellow at the Council on Foreign Relations. He was the Robert E. Wilhelm fellow at the Massachusetts Institute of Technology's Center for International Studies from 2015 to 2016, and later served as an adjunct professor at George Washington University's Elliott School of International Affairs and as a distinguished fellow at the Center for the National Interest. Heer is the author of *Mr. X and the Pacific: George F. Kennan and American Policy in East Asia.*

Charles Hooper served in the U.S. Army for forty-one years, where he held several high-level positions, including U.S. defense attaché in China and Egypt, senior strategist and planner for U.S. Africa Command, deputy strategy director for U.S. Indo-Pacific Command, senior China and Taiwan policy official in the Office of the Secretary of Defense, and director of the Defense Security Cooperation Agency. He also had operational assignments with the 25th Infantry and 82nd Airborne Divisions and taught Chinese foreign policy at the Naval Postgraduate School. Hooper serves on the board of the National Bureau of Asian Research, is a senior fellow at Harvard Kennedy School's Belfer Center for Science and International Affairs, and is a senior nonresident scholar at the Atlantic Council. He holds a certificate in Chinese language and literature from the British Ministry of Defense Chinese Language School and was a postgraduate research fellow at Harvard University's Weatherhead Center for International Affairs. Hooper is a graduate of the U.S. Military Academy at West Point and also Harvard Kennedy School, where he received the Don K. Price Award for Academic Excellence and Public Service.

Ivan Kanapathy is a vice president at Beacon Global Strategies (BGS). Prior to joining BGS, he was a career military officer and foreign affairs practitioner focused on the Indo-Pacific region. From 2018 to 2021, Kanapathy served on the White House's National Security Council staff as deputy senior director for Asian affairs and director for China, Taiwan, and Mongolia. As a military attaché at the American Institute in Taiwan from 2014 to 2017, he represented U.S. interests and advised top U.S. and Taiwanese officials on cross-strait military and security issues. Previously, Kanapathy served as a Marine Corps foreign area officer in China and an F/A-18 instructor at TOPGUN. He is the recipient of the Air Medal, the Navy Marine Corps Commendation Medal with Combat "V," and the Defense Superior Service Medal. Kanapathy is an adjunct professor at Georgetown University's Edmund A. Walsh School of Foreign Service, a senior associate at the Center for Strategic and International Studies, and a senior fellow at the Center for Strategic and Budgetary Assessments. He holds a BS in physics and economics from Carnegie Mellon University, an AA in Chinese-Mandarin from the Defense Language Institute, and an MA in East Asia security studies from the Naval Postgraduate School.

Patricia M. Kim is a David M. Rubenstein fellow at the Brookings Institution and holds a joint appointment to the John L. Thornton China Center and the Center for East Asia Policy Studies. She is an expert on Chinese foreign policy, U.S.-China relations, and regional security dynamics in East Asia. Previously, Dr. Kim served as a China specialist at the U.S. Institute of Peace, where she focused on China's impact on conflict dynamics around the world. She was also a Stanton nuclear security fellow at the Council on Foreign Relations, international security research fellow at the Harvard Kennedy School's Belfer Center for Science and International Affairs, and a postdoctoral fellow at the Princeton-Harvard China and the World Program at Princeton University. Dr. Kim has been published widely in outlets such as *Foreign Affairs, Foreign Policy*, the *New York Times*, and the *Washington Post*, and has testified before the House Intelligence Committee and the House Foreign Affairs Subcommittee on Terrorism, Nonproliferation, and Trade. She received a bachelor's degree from the University of California, Berkeley, and a doctorate from Princeton University.

Margaret K. Lewis is a professor of law at Seton Hall University. Her research focuses on China and Taiwan with an emphasis on criminal justice and human rights as well as on legal issues in the U.S.-China relationship. Lewis has been a Fulbright senior scholar at National Taiwan University, a visiting professor at Academia Sinica, a public intellectuals program fellow with the National Committee on United States-China Relations, a consultant to the Ford Foundation, and a delegate to the U.S.-Japan Foundation's U.S.-Japan Leadership Program. She is also a nonresident affiliated scholar of the New York University (NYU) School of Law's U.S.-Asia Law Institute. In addition to her publications in academic legal journals, Lewis coauthored the book *Challenge to China: How Taiwan Abolished Its Version of Re-Education Through Labor* with Jerome A. Cohen. She received her BA from Columbia University and her JD from NYU. She also studied at the Hopkins-Nanjing Center for Chinese and American Studies.

Chris Miller is an associate professor of international history at Tufts University's Fletcher School of Law and Diplomacy, where his research focuses on technology, geopolitics, economics, international affairs, and Russia. He is author of *Chip War: The Fight for the World's Most Critical Technology*; *Putinomics: Power and Money in Resurgent Russia*; *We Shall Be Masters: Russian Pivots to East Asia From Peter the Great to Putin*; and *The Struggle to Save the Soviet Economy: Mikhail Gorbachev and the Collapse of the USSR*. Miller has previously served as the associate director of Yale University's Brady-Johnson Program in Grand Strategy, a lecturer at the New Economic School in Moscow, a visiting researcher at the Carnegie Moscow Center, a research associate at the Brookings Institution, and a fellow at the German Marshall Fund's Transatlantic Academy. He received his BA in history from Harvard University and his MA and PhD from Yale University.

Michael G. Mullen is the president of MGM Consulting, which provides counsel to global clients on issues related to geopolitical developments, national security interests, and strategic leadership. He previously served as chairman of the U.S. Joint Chiefs of Staff from 2007 to 2011 and as the U.S. Navy's chief of naval operations from 2005 to 2007. Mullen advanced the rapid fielding of innovative technologies, championed emerging and enduring global partnerships, and promoted new methods for countering terrorism. He spearheaded the elimination of the "Don't Ask, Don't Tell" policy, ushering in for the first time in U.S. military history the open service of gay and lesbian men and women.

Meghan L. O'Sullivan is the Jeane Kirkpatrick professor of the practice of international affairs at Harvard Kennedy School and the incoming director of Harvard Kennedy School's Belfer Center for Science and International Affairs. She is a partner at the strategic advisory firm Macro Advisory Partners and the North American chair of the Trilateral Commission. An educator, author, and advisor to companies, O'Sullivan has also served as deputy national security advisor for Iraq and Afghanistan under President George W. Bush, a policy planner under former Secretary of State Colin Powell, and vice chair of the All-Party Talks in Northern Ireland. She is on the board of Raytheon Technologies, of the Council on Foreign Relations, and of nonprofits addressing veterans, conflict, and energy and climate. O'Sullivan is a member of Secretary of State Antony Blinken's Foreign Affairs Policy Board. She holds a bachelor's degree from Georgetown University and a master's degree and doctorate from Oxford University.

Douglas H. Paal is a distinguished fellow at the Carnegie Endowment for International Peace. Between 2006 and 2008, he served as vice chairman of JPMorgan Chase International. From 2002 to 2006, Paal was an unofficial U.S. representative to Taiwan as director of the American Institute in Taiwan. He served on the National Security Council staffs of Presidents Ronald Reagan and George H.W. Bush between 1986 and 1993 as director of Asian affairs and then as senior director and special assistant to the president. Paal held positions in the policy planning staff at the U.S. Department of State, as a senior analyst for the CIA, and at U.S. embassies in Singapore and Beijing. He holds an AM and AB in Chinese studies and Asian history from Brown University and a PhD in history and East Asian languages from Harvard University.

Minxin Pei is the Tom and Margot Pritzker '72 professor of government and George R. Roberts fellow at Claremont McKenna College. He is also a nonresident senior fellow of the German Marshall Fund of the United States. In 2019, Pei served as the inaugural Library of Congress chair on U.S.-China relations. Prior to joining Claremont McKenna College in 2009, he was a senior associate at the Carnegie Endowment for International Peace from 1999 to 2009 and served as director of its China program from 2003 to 2008. Between 1992 and 1998, Pei was an assistant professor of politics at Princeton University. He is the author of *From Reform to Revolution: The Demise of Communism in China and the Soviet Union*; *China's Trapped Transition: The Limits of Developmental Autocracy*; *China's Crony Capitalism: The Dynamics of Regime Decay*;

and *Guarding Dictatorship: China's Surveillance State* (forthcoming). Pei is an opinion columnist for Bloomberg. He has also written for Project Syndicate, *Nikkei Asian Review*, the *Financial Times*, the *New York Times*, the *Washington Post*, the *Wall Street Journal*, and many other news outlets. He received his BA from Shanghai International Studies University and PhD from Harvard University.

Matt Pottinger is a distinguished visiting fellow at Stanford University's Hoover Institution and chairman of the China program at the Foundation for Defense of Democracies. Between 2017 and 2021, Pottinger served at the White House in senior roles on the National Security Council staff, including as senior director for Asia and then as deputy national security advisor. Prior to serving in these roles, he led an Asia-focused risk consultancy and led Asia research at an investment fund in New York. Between 2007 and 2010, Pottinger served as a U.S. Marine in Iraq and Afghanistan. He spent the late 1990s and early 2000s in China as a reporter for Reuters and the *Wall Street Journal*.

Daniel R. Russel is the vice president for international security and diplomacy at the Asia Society Policy Institute (ASPI), where he also previously served as a diplomat in residence and senior fellow for a one-year term. He most recently served as the assistant secretary of state for East Asian and Pacific affairs from 2013 to 2017. Prior to that role, Russel served as special assistant to the president and National Security Council senior director for Asian affairs at the White House, where he helped formulate President Barack Obama's strategic rebalance to the Asia Pacific region. Before that, he served in several positions as part of the Senior Foreign Service at the U.S. Department of State. Russel is a recipient of the State Department's Una Chapman Cox Foundation fellowship sabbatical. Before joining the Foreign Service, he was a manager for an international firm in New York City. He is the author of *America's Place in the World*. Russel was educated at Sarah Lawrence College and the University of London.

David Sacks is a research fellow at the Council on Foreign Relations, where his work focuses on U.S.-Taiwan relations, U.S.-China relations, Chinese foreign policy, cross-strait relations, and the political thought of Hans Morgenthau. He directed the CFR-sponsored Independent Task Force on China's Belt and Road Initiative, chaired by Jack Lew and Gary Roughead. Prior to joining CFR, Sacks worked on political military affairs at the American Institute in Taiwan. Sacks was also a Princeton in Asia fellow in Hangzhou, China. He received a bachelor's degree in political science from Carleton College and a master's degree in international relations and international economics, with honors, from the Johns Hopkins University's School of Advanced International Studies (SAIS). At SAIS, he was the recipient of the A. Doak Barnett Award, given annually to the most distinguished China studies graduate.

TASK FORCE OBSERVERS

Observers participate in Task Force discussions but are not asked to join the consensus. They participate in their individual, not institutional, capacities.

Christa N. Almonte is a captain in the U.S. Navy and a foreign area officer specializing in both the Middle East and Indo-Pacific. She served as the naval attaché and chief of attaché operations to Saudi Arabia from 2019 to 2021. From 2015 to 2017, Almonte served at United States Indo-Pacific Command at Camp H. M. Smith, first as a strategic contingency planner for operations within East and Southeast Asia and subsequently as the executive assistant to the director of strategic planning and policy (J5). In the Pentagon, she served as the Middle East desk officer monitoring navy foreign policy within the Levant and Pakistan, and, subsequently, as the deputy executive assistant for the deputy chief of naval operations for operations, plans, and strategy. During two tours in Bahrain, Almonte served as a navy security cooperation officer at the U.S. embassy, and as Tomahawk strike officer on the Destroyer Squadron staff at the onset of the Iraq War. Almonte holds master's degrees from George Washington University, the Naval War College, and the Joint Advanced Warfighting School and an associate's degree in Arabic from the Defense Language Institute Foreign Language Center.

Robert D. Blackwill is the Henry A. Kissinger senior fellow for U.S. foreign policy at the Council on Foreign Relations and a member of Harvard Kennedy School's Applied History Project. He previously served as deputy assistant to the president and deputy national security advisor for strategic planning under President George W. Bush from 2003 to 2004, where he also served as presidential envoy to Iraq. Prior to those roles, Blackwill served as U.S. ambassador to India from 2001 to 2003. Before that, he was the Belfer lecturer in international security at Harvard Kennedy School, where he was also associate dean and faculty chair for executive training programs for foreign leaders. Between 1989 and 1990, Blackwill was special assistant to President George H.W. Bush for European and Soviet affairs. He has also served as U.S. ambassador to conventional arms negotiations with the Warsaw Pact, director for European affairs at the National Security Council, principal deputy assistant secretary of state for political-military affairs, and principal deputy assistant secretary of state for European affairs. Blackwill is the recipient of the Bridge-Builder Award, the Padma Bhushan Award, and the Commander's Cross of the Order of Merit. He is the author of *War by Other Means: Geoeconomics and Statecraft*; *Lee Kuan Yew: The Grand Master's Insights on China, the United States, and the World*; and the Council Special Report *The United States, China, and Taiwan: A Strategy to Prevent War*. Blackwill holds a BA from Wichita State University.

Ian Johnson is the Stephen A. Schwarzman senior fellow for China studies at the Council on Foreign Relations. Prior to that role, he worked as a journalist in China and Germany, writing for publications such as the *Wall Street Journal*, the *New York Times*, the *New York Review of Books*, and the *Baltimore Sun*. Johnson is a contributor to the CFR blog *Asia Unbound* and a frequent contributor to media outlets in the United States. He is the recipient of a Pulitzer Prize, two Overseas Press Club awards, Stanford University's Shorenstein Journalism Award, and awards from both the Society of Professional Journalists and the American Academy of Religion. He is the author of *The Souls of China: The Return of Religion After Mao*; *Wild Grass: Three Stories of Change in Modern China*; and *A Mosque in Munich: Nazis, the CIA, and the Rise of the Muslim Brotherhood in the West*. Johnson has received research and writing grants from the Open Society Foundation, the Pulitzer Center on Crisis Reporting, the Alicia Patterson Foundation, and the Robert B. Silvers Foundation. He was also awarded a 2020–21 National Endowment for the Humanities Public Scholars fellowship for a new book he is writing on China's unofficial history.

Manjari Chatterjee Miller is a senior fellow for India, Pakistan, and South Asia at the Council on Foreign Relations. She is also a research associate in the contemporary South Asian studies program at the University of Oxford's Oxford School of Global and Area Studies. Miller is currently on leave from Boston University's Frederick S. Pardee School of Global Studies, where she is a tenured associate professor of international relations and the director of the Pardee Center's Rising Powers Initiative. She has been a nonresident fellow at the Atlantic Council, a fellow at the Harvard Kennedy School's Belfer Center for Science and International Affairs, a visiting associate professor at the National University of Singapore's Lee Kuan Yew School of Public Policy, and a visiting scholar at the Chinese Academy of Social Sciences and Australian National University's Crawford School of Public Policy. She is the author of *Why Nations Rise: Narratives and the Path to Great Power* and *Wronged by Empire: Post-Imperial Ideology and Foreign Policy in India and China*. Miller is also the coeditor of the *Routledge Handbook of China-India Relations*, writes as a monthly columnist for the *Hindustan Times*, and is a frequent contributor to policy and media outlets in the United States and Asia. She serves on the international advisory board of Chatham House's *International Affairs* journal. Miller received a BA from the University of Delhi, an MSc from the University of London, and a PhD from Harvard University.

Carl F. Minzner is a senior fellow for China studies at the Council on Foreign Relations. He is also a professor at the Fordham University School of Law, specializing in Chinese politics and law. Prior to teaching at Fordham, Minzner was an associate professor at the School of Law at Washington University in St. Louis. From 2003 to 2006, he was senior counsel at the Congressional-Executive Commission on China, where he monitored, reported, and advised on rule-of-law and human rights issues in the People's Republic of China for both Congress and the executive branch. He has served as a Fulbright scholar; a fellow in the Public Intellectuals Program at the National Committee on U.S.-China Relations; a Yale-China Association legal education fellow at the Northwest Institute of Politics and Law in Xi'an, China; a law clerk for the Honorable Raymond Clevenger of the U.S. Court of Appeals for the Federal Circuit; and a teacher with Volunteers in Asia in Tainan, China. Minzner is the author of *End of an Era: How China's Authoritarian Revival Is Undermining Its Rise*. He has published numerous articles on Chinese politics and governance in academic publications including *China Quarterly, Asia Policy*, the *American Journal of Comparative Law*, the *Journal of Democracy*, and *China Leadership Monitor*, as well as opinion pieces in the *New York Times*, the *Los Angeles Times*, and the *Christian Science Monitor*, among others. Minzner received a BA in international relations from Stanford University, an MIA from Columbia University's School of International and Public Affairs, and a JD from Columbia Law School. He is a member of the State Bar of California.

Nargiza Salidjanova is the director of the China projects team at the Rhodium Group, where she leads the firm's integrated analysis of China's economic system, technology development, and global engagement. She previously served as director for economics and trade at the U.S.-China Economic and Security Review Commission. Salidjanova has published on a broad range of topics, including strategic competition, China's role in global governance, and the alignment of commerce and national security concerns. She holds a master's degree in international economic policy with a concentration on China from American University.

Anya Schmemann (ex officio) is the managing director of global communications and outreach and director of the Independent Task Force program at the Council on Foreign Relations in Washington, DC. At CFR, Schmemann has overseen numerous high-level Task Forces on a wide range of topics, including cybersecurity, China's Belt and Road Initiative, pandemic preparedness, innovation, the future of work, Arctic strategy, nuclear weapons, climate change, immigration, trade policy, and internet governance, as well as on U.S. policy toward Afghanistan, Brazil, North Korea, Pakistan, and Turkey. She previously served as assistant dean for communications and outreach at American University's School of International Service and managed communications at Harvard Kennedy School's Belfer Center for Science and International Affairs, where she also administered the Caspian Studies Program. She coordinated a research project on Russian security issues at the East-West Institute in New York and was assistant director of CFR's Center for Preventive Action in New York, focusing on the Balkans and Central Asia. She was a Truman National Security Fellow and is co-chair of the Global Kids DC advisory council. Schmemann received a BA in government and an MA in Russian studies from Harvard University.

Sheila A. Smith is the John E. Merow senior fellow for Asia-Pacific studies at the Council on Foreign Relations. Prior to this role, she was a fellow at the East-West Center in Washington, DC, where she directed a multinational research team in a cross-national study of the domestic politics of the U.S. military presence in Japan, the Philippines, and South Korea. Between 2007 and 2008, Smith was a visiting scholar at Keio University in Tokyo. She has been a visiting researcher at the Japan Institute of International Affairs, the Research Institute for Peace and Security, the University of Tokyo, and the University of the Ryukyus. Smith is chair of the Japan-U.S. Friendship Commission and the U.S. advisors to the U.S.-Japan Conference on Cultural and Educational Interchange. She teaches as an adjunct professor at Georgetown University and serves on the board of its *Journal of Asian Affairs*. Smith also serves on the advisory committee for the U.S.-Japan Network for the Future program at the Maureen and Mike Mansfield Foundation. She is the author of *Japan Rearmed: The Politics of Military Power*; *Intimate Rivals: Japanese Domestic Politics and a Rising China*; and *Japan's New Politics and the U.S.-Japan Alliance*. She earned her MA and PhD from Columbia University.

Erin M. Staine-Pyne is a colonel in the U.S. Air Force, and most recently served as the senior military advisor to the undersecretary of the air force. She is a command pilot and graduate of the U.S. Air Force Weapons School, with more than 3,400 flight hours in mobility aircraft, including combat airdrop missions over Afghanistan. Staine-Pyne has served in staff assignments at the major command, sub-unified command, and combatant command levels. She has commanded both an in-garrison airlift squadron as well as a deployed expeditionary squadron for Operation Iraqi Freedom and Operation Inherent Resolve. Staine-Pyne served as the wing commander, 62nd Airlift Wing, at Joint Base Lewis McChord in Washington State. She earned a bachelor's degree from the United States Air Force Academy, a master's degree in public administration from the University of Colorado, and a master's degree in national security strategy from the National Defense University.

Contributing CFR Staff

Dalia Albarrán
Associate Director,
Graphic Design

Maria Teresa Alzuru
Deputy Director,
Product Management

Sabine Baumgartner
Senior Photo Editor

Michael Bricknell
Data Visualization Designer

Patricia Lee Dorff
Managing Director, Publications

Seaton Huang
Research Associate, Asia Studies

Will Merrow
Associate Director,
Data Visualization

Caitlin Moran
Senior Editor,
Publications

Anya Schmemann
Managing Director,
Independent Task Force Program

Chelie Setzer
Deputy Director,
Independent Task Force Program

Connor Sutherland
Program Coordinator,
Washington Meetings and
Independent Task Force Program

Contributing Interns

Robin Brinkmann
Independent Task Force Program

David Brostoff
Asia Studies,
International Relations Theory

Addis Goldman
Asia Studies,
International Relations Theory

Claire Tiunn (Chang)
Independent Task Force Program

Keely Thompson
Independent Task Force Program